The Cholmondeley Ladies

The Cholmondeley Ladies
c.1600–10
BRITISH SCHOOL

Look at the two women. Can you spot the differences between them? How are they related?

Where are the women sitting? Why are they shown there?

The picture was painted to celebrate something. Can you tell what? A clue is some writing in the picture, bottom left.

What sort of a family do you think the Cholmondeleys were?

Can you work out why the babies are so stiff and straight?

How old is this painting? What clues help you tell its age?

Find a picture in this room which was made later. Compare the way the figures have been painted.

What colours do you see in this painting? What is the effect of using so few colours?

Can you think of any reasons why we don't know the artist's name?

FURTHER INFORMATION

The women look like twins. However, the historian John T. Hopkins believes that

> 'the women were not twins and there were a few years between their ages, but they may have shared the same birthday. They may both have been married in the same chapel. Their first born children were perhaps born on the same date. It is likely that their (the women's) widowed mother commissioned and paid for a commemorative portrait of the two births, painted in 1606 or 1607 by a Chester artist.'

The written explanation on the picture was a great simplification. It was added 150 years later. Think about how family stories change and become less accurate over time.

Historians can tell who families are by the signs and patterns included in their portraits. For example, look at the embroidered panels on the ladies' dresses. These emblems or crests would have been easily recognised by others at the time. Notice that the babies have the same patterns as their mothers. This is because their mothers married into different families.

It is possible to tell that this was made in the early seventeenth century, from the stiff, stylised way in which it has been painted and because it is painted on wood panel (rather than on canvas as were later pictures). Other clues include the details of their costumes and hairstyles. At this time, babies were swaddled or tightly wrapped up. These babies are wearing christening gowns over their swaddling.

The artist's name is not known because painters rarely signed their work at this time. Painters were regarded as craftsmen, working in guilds.

 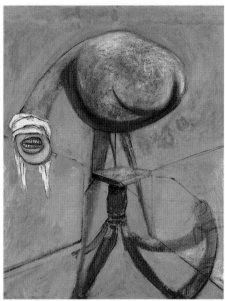 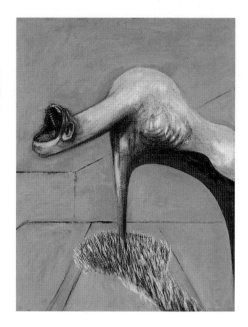

Three Studies for Figures at the Base of a Crucifixion *c.*1944
FRANCIS BACON 1909–1992

What do these 'figures' look like to you? Which parts are human and which are animal? Why do none of the figures have eyes?

Where are the figures? (Describe the space and position of the figures.)

Where do you think Bacon found ideas for these figures?

What is a triptych? Where would you find more traditional examples of triptych paintings?

Look closely at the way Bacon has painted the three panels – describe the textures and brushstrokes.

This work was painted in 1944 during the Second World War. What sort of statement could Bacon be making about the war? Imagine how viewers then would have reacted to this work.

FURTHER INFORMATION

This work combines three part-animal/part-human figures against a background of strong orange to create a powerful and disturbing image. The work refers to the subject of the Crucifixion and the triptych format of traditional Western religious painting. Bacon chose this subject, a portrayal of human suffering, to explore his own vision of man. He was fascinated by the idea of painting a scream.

The artist also stated that the figures make reference to the Greek Furies, the instruments of vengeance of the Greek gods, described in Classical literature. Other sources for the work include high-speed photography, a book on diseases of the mouth, the writings of the ex-surrealist Georges Bataille, and a still from the Russian film by Sergei Eisenstein, *Battleship Potemkin* (1925), showing in close-up the face of a screaming woman who has just been shot.

'You could say that a scream is a horrific image; in fact I wanted to paint the scream more than the horror. I think, if I had really thought about what causes somebody to scream, it would have made the scream that I had tried to paint more successful. In fact they were too abstract.' (Bacon)

'I would like my pictures to look as if a human being has passed through them, like a snail, leaving a trail of the human presence and memory traces of past events, as the snail leaves its slime.' (Bacon)

An A–Z of Displays 1997

This guide is based on projected display plans and is correct at the time of writing. Please telephone the Information Office on 0171 887 8734 to confirm details. An updated guide will be available from May 1998 which can be sent free of charge when you telephone Tate Education on 0171 887 8887.

You can also refer to the *TatePlan*, updated monthly and available free in the Gallery.

Rm = Room number
TBC = To be confirmed
Duveens = central sculpture halls

A

- *The Age of Confidence: 1760–1800* Rm 3 (Until November 1997)
- *Apocalypse and Pastoral: Neo Romanticism in England* Rm 19 (1 April 1997–February 1998)
- Jean Arp Rm 17
- Michael Ayrton Rm 19

B

- Francis Bacon Rm 20
- Vanessa Bell Rm 15
- *William Blake and the Ancients* Rm 7 (Until 22 July 1997)
- *William Blake in Focus Exhibition* Rm 7 (4 August– 26 October 1997) TBC
- *Britannia's Realm: Coastal Themes 1880–1910* Rm 11 (6 May–November 1997)
- Umberto Boccioni Rm 14
- David Bomberg Rm 14
- Pierre Bonnard Rm 13
- Georges Braque Rm 14, Rm 21
- Stephen Buckley Rm 25 (4 August–October 1997) TBC
- Sir Edward Burne-Jones Rm 9

C

- Patrick Caulfield (Prints) Rm 25 (Until late July 1997)
- Paul Cézanne Rm 14
- Marc Chagall Rm 12
- *A Clear Vision* Rm 18 (7 April 1997–February 1998)
- Sir William Coldstream Rm 15
- Cecil Collins Rm 12, Rm 19
- *Colour as Form: Abstract Painting in the 1950s* Rm 23 (14 April 1997–February 1998)
- *Constable and his Contemporaries: Landscape Painting 1800–1850* Rm 8 (Until November 1997)
- Tony Cragg: Duveen Sculpture galleries (From late July 1997)

D

- Salvador Dalí Rm 17
- *The Decorative Impulse: Late Impressionism and Its Legacy* Rm 13 (12 May–November 1997)
- Edgar Degas Rm 13
- Robert Delaunay Rm 14
- André Derain Rm 14
- Theo van Doesburg Rm 17
- *Drawn from Life: British Art 1905–40* Rm 15 (28 April–November 1997)
- *Dreams and Visions: From Redon to Chagall* Rm 12 (6 May–November 1997)
- Jean Dubuffet Rm 20

E

- Sir Jacob Epstein: Duveens, Rm 14, Rm 15 (From late July 1997)
- Max Ernst Rm 17
- *Evocations of Nature: Abstract Painting since 1945* Rm 24 (17 March–21 July 1997)
- *The Experience of Place: Painting in St Ives 1956–60* Rm 24 (4 August–October 1997) TBC

F

- Luciano Fabro: Duveen Sculpture Galleries (11 February–15 June 1997)
- Barry Flanagan: Duveens (From late July 1997)
- Lucio Fontana Rm 21
- Meredith Frampton Rm 15, Rm 18
- Lucian Freud Rm 18, Rm 19
- Froehlich: Baselitz and Kiefer Rm 26, Rm 27 (10 June–October 1997) TBC
- Froehlich: Baselitz and Kiefer (Prints) Rm 28 (10 June–October 1997) TBC
- Terry Frost Rm 24 (From August 1997)

G

- Thomas Gainsborough Rm 3, Rm 4
- Henri Gaudier-Brzeska: Duveens, Rm 15 (From late July 1997)
- Giacometti, Bacon and Dubuffet Rm 20 (21 April 1997–February 1998)
- *Alfred Gilbert and the New Sculpture – Ambulatories* (7 April 1997–Spring 1998)
- Eric Gill: Duveens (From late July 1997)
- Harold Gilman Rm 15
- *The Great Debate: Surrealism vs Abstraction* Rm 17 (28 April 1997–February 1998)

H

- Richard Hamilton (Prints) Rm 25 (Until late July 1997)
- Dame Barbara Hepworth: Duveens (From late July 1997)
- Patrick Heron Rm 23, Rm 24 (From August 1997)
- Nicholas Hilliard Rm 1
- Roger Hilton Rm 24 (From August 1997)
- William Holman Hunt Rm 10
- Hans Hoffman Rm 23
- *Hogarth's London* Rm 2 (Closed 16–20 June for changes)
- *At Home and Abroad: Landscape Watercolours and Drawings c.1750–1870* Rm 5 (Until November 1997)

I

- *Image and Allegory: Tudor and Stuart Painting* Rm 1 (Until November 1997)

J

- Augustus and Gwen John Rm 15

K

- Wassily Kandinsky Rm 14, Rm 17
- Anish Kapoor: Duveens (From late July 1997)
- *Ellsworth Kelly*: Major Exhibition (12 June– 7 September 1997)
- Paul Klee Rm 12

L

- Sir Edwin Landseer Rm 9
- Peter Lanyon Rm 24 (From August 1997)
- Sir Thomas Lawrence Rm 3
- Fernand Léger Rm 17
- Lord Frederic Leighton Rm 9
- Wyndham Lewis Rm 15
- *The Loire*: Clore Gallery (30 October 1997–?)

M

- René Magritte Rm 17
- Henri Matisse Rm 14, Rm 23
- John Everett Millais Rm 9, Rm 10, Rm 11
- John Minton Rm 19
- Joan Miró Rm 17
- Henry Moore: Duveens, Rm 17 (From late July 1997)

N

- Paul Nash Rm 19
- Barnett Newman Rm 23
- Ben Nicholson Rm 17, Rm 21

P

- Eduardo Paolozzi (Prints) Rm 25 (Until late July 1997)
- Pablo Picasso Rm 14, Rm 17
- John Piper Rm 19
- Camille Pissarro Rm 13
- Pollock and Smith Rm 22 (14 April 1997–February 1998)
- *The Pre-Raphaelite Brotherhood and Its Influence* Rm 10 (Closed 23–27 June for changes)

R

- *Reality and Imagination in the Eighteenth Century Landscape* Rm 4 (Until November 1997)
- *Redefining Art: Radical Movements 1900–1920* Rm 14 (19 May–November 1997)
- Odilon Redon Rm 12
- Auguste Renoir Rm 13
- Sir Joshua Reynolds Rm 3
- William Roberts Rm 15
- Dante Gabriel Rossetti Rm 9
- Mark Rothko Rm 23
- Rothko Rm 29 (Until 15 September 1997) TBC

S

- John Singer Sargent Rm 9
- Karl Schmidt-Rottluff Rm 14
- *Sculpture in Stone*: Duveen Sculpture Galleries (23 July 1997–January 1998)
- Kurt Schwitters Rm 17
- Gino Severini Rm 14
- Walter Sickert Rm 15
- David Smith Rm 22, Rm 23
- Sir Matthew Smith Rm 15
- Sir Stanley Spencer Rm 15, Rm 18
- Philip Wilson Steer Rm 11
- George Stubbs Rm 3, Rm 4
- Graham Sutherland Rm 19

T

- *Henry Tate Centenary Display*: Special Displays Rm 1, Rm 2 (1 July–19 October 1997)
- *Texture, Surface and Space: European Art of the 1950s* Rm 21 (21 April 1997–February 1998)
- *Town and Country: Sporting Art and Genre* Pictures Rm 6 (Until November 1997)
- Francis Towne: Clore Galleries 111–112 (24 June– 14 September 1997)

V

- Victorian Painting Rm 9 (Closed 23–27 June for changes)
- Edouard Vuillard Rm 13

W

- Edward Wadsworth Rm 17, Rm 18
- George Watts Rm 9
- James Abbott McNeill Whistler Rm 11
- Joseph Wright of Derby Rm 3, Rm 4
- Bryan Wynter Rm 24 (From August 1997)

Flatford Mill ('Scene on a Navigable River') 1816–17
JOHN CONSTABLE 1776–1837

Describe what is going on and name the different jobs the people are doing.

Was Constable painting a scene of his own time or in the past? Give reasons for your opinion.

Do you think it was painted outdoors in front of an actual scene or invented in the artist's studio? How can you tell?

What time of year and time of day is it? How do you know?

Look at the way the artist has applied the paint. How has he captured the physical earthiness of the land?

Take two contrasting areas, such as the clouds and tree trunks. Make two sketches that show the colours, textures and brushstrokes Constable uses for each.

FURTHER INFORMATION

John Constable is the most famous painter of the English countryside. He developed almost scientific ways of painting the landscape naturalistically. However, the paintings often show an idealised vision of happy, busy labourers toiling in a fruitful, well-ordered landscape. In reality, a rural life was often hard and unrewarding.

This scene, as with all his works, was contemporary to Constable and not historical. At this time landscape painting was still considered inferior to 'History' and 'Portrait' painting. Constable did make a number of portraits but his abiding passion was rural England. Constable was born and grew up in the countryside shown in this painting, which was an area on the borders of Essex and Suffolk. His father owned Flatford Mill and the family also owned a boatyard that built barges and maintained the lock gates. All these experiences influenced the artist's vision of the countryside.

At this time, most landscape paintings were created in the studio from preparatory studies (including those of Constable), but this quite large canvas was painted mainly outdoors, some fifty years before the Impressionists adopted the same *plein air* practice.

The thick, earthy browns and greens, capture the solidity and textures of soil, trees and water. He also faithfully records the particular formation of clouds and play of light.

Christ in the House of his Parents

**Christh in the House of his Parents
('The Carpenter's Shop') 1849–50
JOHN EVERETT MILLAIS
1829–1896**

The title tells you that the boy with red hair is Jesus. What has hurt his hand? Who is comforting him?

The blood on his foot foretells the end of Jesus's life. Do you know how he died?

Millais makes the story seem real by painting it in great detail. For example, can you see the dirt under the fingernails? What other details do you notice? (Look at Joseph's arms.) What size brush do you think Millais used?

Individual details or symbols help tell the story. For instance, what does the colour red make you think of? Who could the sheep stand for? The dove on the ladder is there to suggest something biblical. What might that be?

Millais wanted to make you believe that the Bible story was true by making it seem so real that you would feel you were there yourself. Do you? Apart from the details how does he manage to make us feel we are there?

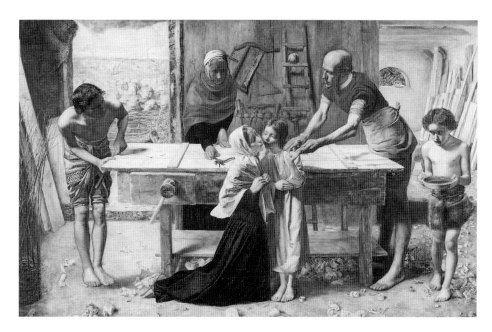

FURTHER INFORMATION

Millais painted this picture when he was twenty. With some friends he had formed the Pre-Raphaelite Brotherhood in 1848 – their aim was to return to the purity of art before Raphael. The Bible and Shakespeare were sources for many of their pictures. They meant these works to be different from the art of the past in that they were to be absolutely true to life. This meant that Millais studied a real carpenter as the model for Joseph, in order to observe his muscular arms and his workbench and tools. But when it came to the carpenter's head, Millais used his father as the model as his domed head was considered, at the time, to indicate a noble and spiritual personality. Such detailed study from life was intended to give a sense of truth so that viewers

could identify with what they saw. The many religious paintings produced in the Renaissance had created a sense of awe. But the Pre-Raphaelites felt that their subject matter and meanings were too overwhelmed by their beauty. They wanted viewers to visualise scenes from the Bible completely freshly. This meant choosing part of the Christian story which had not often been treated before and then painting it as vividly as if it were a new idea. Do you think that this approach works? Was the painting too difficult to read or not?

The Pre-Raphaelites were criticised for painting stories which might have been better written than painted. Sometimes their symbolism is certainly difficult to work out. Did you realise, for instance,

that the triangle on the wall stands for the Holy Trinity and the dove for the Holy Spirit? It is interesting that Dickens disliked this painting intensely. He described Millais's Christchild as a 'hideous, wry-necked, blubbering, red-headed boy, in a bed-gown', and said that the mother was 'horrible in her ugliness'. What upset him and others was the ordinariness of the people. They did not seem beautiful enough to be holy. To him, it was blasphemy to paint from the Bible in the same way that you painted scenes of everyday life.

Lobster Telephone 1936
SALVADOR DALÍ 1904–1989

What is this sculpture made from?

Are there any visual clues to tell you when it was made?

Are the objects real or has the artist made them look real?

Why do you think Dalí chose a lobster?

At the time this object was made what kind of people might have owned a telephone or eaten lobsters?

What would happen if you put the lobster to your ear? What would you feel? What would you hear?

Does the combination of the lobster and the telephone suggest any proverb or phrase to you, for instance, 'sounds fishy'?
Think up your own.

Would a lobster make a good mobile phone? Try designing a Surreal mobile phone. Think of an appropriate object. What impression would it give? How would it be held and used?

FURTHER INFORMATION

Salvador Dalí was a Spanish Surrealist artist who made both paintings and sculpture. Surrealists were interested in stimulating and articulating thoughts and emotions that come from our irrational selves. Surrealist art either recorded subconscious experience, for example, in the form of remembered dreams or, more often, created strange provocative images to arouse the viewer's dormant subconscious. These artists often used actual objects or created super-realistic images to heighten the sense of the bizarre by seeming so 'real'.

Chance
Surrealist artists used different methods to liberate their own and their audience's subconscious. They believed that chance could act as a catalyst in this process, and the nineteenth-century writer Lautreamont (1846–70) spoke of the beauty of 'the chance encounter on a dissecting-table of a sewing-machine and an umbrella'. Surrealists adapted the game Consequences to drawing and called it Exquisite Bodies (*Corps Exquis*). They also chopped up texts and allowed words to fall at random to form new sentences, producing unforeseen and strange narratives.

Readymades
Marcel Duchamp (1887–1968) was the first artist to bring readymade objects into the gallery and exhibit them as art (as a unique creative product, signed by an artist). From 1913 Duchamp explored ideas of taste, the sanctifying nature of the art gallery, physical displacement and the role of the artist in a series of readymades that included a wine rack, a urinal and a bicycle wheel upside down on a stool. Dalí's readymades are different in that they deliberately make punning links between the physical shapes of completely unrelated objects. When brought together these objects start a dialogue whose strange nature taps into the unregulated realms of the viewer's mind.

Head of a Woman (Fernande)
1909
PABLO PICASSO 1881–1973

Look closely at this work from all sides.
What has happened to the head?
Think of words to describe the surfaces
and shapes. Make small sketches of parts
of this head, noting areas which are
sharp, curved, textured, etc.

How do you think the sculpture was
made? (Look for evidence of tool or
finger marks.)

Look around the Gallery for a sculpture
bust by a more 'traditional' artist. How
does Picasso depart from the tradition? Is
this a sculpture of Fernande as an
individual or just a head?

Why do you think Picasso has chosen to
describe the head and hair in the way that
he has?

If possible find a painting by Picasso to
connect with this sculpture. Compare
and contrast the way he has treated the
human form.

FURTHER INFORMATION

This head is based on Picasso's companion at the time, Fernande Olivier. Her
head is described by a series of planes and
curved segments which follow her facial
features and hair.

During this period, Picasso and the
French artist Georges Braque
(1882–1963) were developing their so-
called Cubist paintings which challenged
the idea of single viewpoint perspective.
Picasso's experiments with the two-
dimensional space of the canvas gave him

ideas for three-dimensional work. With
Head of a Woman Picasso explores sculptural space: The work challenges traditional sculpture by breaking down the
outer surface and creating a series of
planes and volumes. The bold shapes and
simplification of form seen in this work
show the influence of African, Oceanic
and Iron-Age European art. Like many
artists at this time, Picasso was interested
in this kind of art.

Picasso made two plaster casts of this

head and at least sixteen bronze versions.
According to his biographer John
Richardson, this version was returned to
Picasso in the 1950s and the artist
remodelled some planes using a knife.

*'Sculpture is the best comment that a
painter can make on his painting.'*
(Picasso)

The Snail

The Snail 1953
HENRI MATISSE 1869–1954

If you can, compare the real thing to a postcard reproduction of it. How does the real thing make you feel?

Can you see the spiral based on a snail shell? What else can you see in the arrangement of shapes?

How do the colours make you feel? Find words to describe each of them.

Do you know what kind of colours Matisse has used? Try covering up the black with your hand to see what job it does.

How was it made? (Clues: pinholes at the corners of each shape; the brush lines; the different edges of each shape.)

Have the shapes been arranged in a deliberate order or do you think they are totally random?

FURTHER INFORMATION

The Snail is one of Matisse's large collages or 'cut-out gouaches' made towards the end of his life. Matisse began to use this technique from 1948 when ill health prevented him from painting at an easel. Helped by assistants, he was able to manipulate paper and scissors to place coloured pieces on background sheets.

Although inspired by the shell of a snail, the work is essentially abstract and its real subject is the exploration of colour. The artist has used the three primary colours and the three secondary colours and he has placed them so that they 'sing' vibrantly together in their complementary relationships.

Matisse was living in the South of France at the time and so this work could be seen as a response to the vivid colour and light of the Mediterranean.

'I first of all drew the snail from nature, holding it. I became aware of an unrolling, I found an image in my mind purified of the shell, then I took the scissors.' (Matisse)

The paper cut-out allows me to draw in colour. It is a simplification for me. Instead of drawing the outline and putting the colour inside it – the one modifying the other – I draw straight into colour.' (Matisse)

Further ideas
Try taking a small object, natural or man-made, and making repeat drawings in order to find the simplest, most abstract way of representing it.

Discuss colour relationships – primary, secondary and complementary colours and the roles of black and white in this work.

Murals for the Seagram Building
1958–9
MARK ROTHKO 1903–1970

Try to be quiet in this room because many people come in here to be peaceful.

How does the room feel to you?

Rothko wanted all these paintings to be shown together and gave certain rules about how they should be displayed. What do you think those rules were?

Chose one painting. Stand well back and then move forward to look really closely at it.
How many layers of paint can you see?
Do you think Rothko is a careful or a messy artist?

Notice some of the paintings have paint drips running upwards.
Why do you think that is? (A clue – the canvas is very big)

Stare at a rectangle in your painting. Can you imagine yourself going through this 'window'? Or does it stay flat?

How many different colours can you see in this room?
Try to describe the different kinds of red.
Can you find any matching pairs of paintings?
Are any of them symmetrical?

FURTHER INFORMATION

These paintings were given to the Tate Gallery in 1969 by the artist on condition that they would hang together in a space of their own without strong lighting. Rothko aimed to create a calm, meditative atmosphere for the viewing of this work; he wanted visitors to be affected by his paintings. The room could be described as a 'total work of art'.

These huge dark canvases were originally intended to decorate the Four Seasons restaurant in New York, but Rothko felt that they had a contemplative, even spiritual quality which made them quite unsuitable for a fashionable and expensive restaurant. He later painted a similar group of murals for a chapel in Houston, Texas.

'After I had been at work for some time I realised that I was much influenced subconsciously by Michelangelo's walls in the staircase of the Medicean Library in Florence. He achieved just the kind of feeling I am after.' (Rothko referring to the blank stone windows set in the white walls of the ante-room of the Laurentian Library.)

'I paint large pictures because I want to create a state of intimacy. A large picture is an immediate transaction: it takes you into it.' (Rothko)

Forest and Dove 1927
MAX ERNST 1891–1976

Is this an image of a real or imaginary
forest?

Imagine if you were ant-sized in that
forest!

What is the mood of this picture?

Does it stir any memories of dreams or
similar places? Do the tree shapes remind
you of anything else?

Do you think the bird is free or in a cage?

If this picture has meaning to the artist,
what do you think the dove and the forest
might mean?

Can you work out how the artist made
this painting? What tools, materials and
techniques has he used?

FURTHER INFORMATION

Max Ernst grew up near a forest
and never forgot the enchantment and
terror he felt when his father first took
him into it.

When a small boy, Ernst had a pink
cockatoo as a pet. He was very upset
when it died and invented a fantasy bird
which he called Loplop. Birds became an
important symbol in his paintings.

Ernst was a German-born painter,
sculptor and printmaker, and a leading
Surrealist. Surrealists created imaginative
works involving irrational combinations
of imagery, often inspired by dreams or
chance happenings.

Many of Ernst's works feature bizarre,
fossilised landscapes and creatures, that
evoke both pre-history and a 'sci-fi'
future. In 1934 he wrote a story 'The
Mysteries of the Forest' in which he
imagined a future when forests had lost
their enchantment due to human inter-
ference and destruction. These concerns,
also embodied in his paintings, speak to
our current anxieties about ecology and
the plight of the rain forests.

Once, Ernst found himself staring at
the patterns of the grain in some wooden
floorboards. He discovered that by covering the wood with paper and rubbing

over it with a pencil, the patterns
appeared on the paper. By experimenting
he soon discovered how to make paintings in a similar way.

He called this new technique frottage
(from the French word *frotter* meaning 'to
rub'). It enabled him to make completely
imaginative pictures. He has used
frottage to create this painting. In some
places he has also scratched into the surface, for example, the cage and parts of
the bird.

**Mrs Mounter at the Breakfast
Table exhibited 1917
HAROLD GILMAN 1876–1919**

How old do you think Mrs Mounter is?
What kind of life has she led?
How does she feel?

Would you like to be eating breakfast in
that room?
What do you like / dislike about the
interior decoration?

How does the painting make you feel?

Is there anything about Mrs Mounter
or her room which tells you that this is
London and not Europe?

What do you know about the age in
which this was painted? How might this
connect with its mood?

Look at the colours and patterns from a
distance. Now move closer to the picture.
How different do they look from both
distances? What unusual colours do you
see in her face?

FURTHER INFORMATION

Harold Gilman was a follower of Walter
Sickert, who encouraged him to paint
'nudes on a bed, at their toilet, or just
naturally inhabiting their shabby bedsit-
ters in Camden Town … and landscapes
of commonplace London streets, squares
and gardens.' Then in 1910, he was enor-
mously excited by an exhibition called
Manet and the Post Impressionists. From
then on, although his subject matter did
not change very much, his way of painting changed, inspired by the example of
Vincent van Gogh. In his portraits van
Gogh had focused on ordinary people,
whom he considered to be the salt of the

earth. He had emphasised their human
qualities, portraying them full face, gaz-
ing straight into our eyes. Gilman does
the same with Mrs Mounter, who was his
landlady in Camden. He shows her in a
typically British interior sitting at a table,
set with a standard brown teapot, a lus-
treware milk jug and two plain,
unmatched, white teacups. Alone, sad
but dogged, she reminds us of the
women left at home by soldiers gone to
fight in the First World War.

Gilman admired the bright colours
used by van Gogh when he was in the
South of France but these were not

suitable for the English climate. Instead
of Vincent's whirling brushstrokes,
Gilman applied paint in small patches of
colour as if he were assembling a mosaic.
Close to, Mrs Mounter's face is a patch-
work of mauve, orange, green and pink
which blend with one another to create
an impression of flesh colouring from a
distance.

Mrs Mounter looks determined to sur-
vive the harsh wartime period, but her
painter died in his early forties in the
terrible epidemic of influenza in 1919.

Looking into the Tate

Exciting Ways to Explore the Tate Gallery's Collection

Written and edited by Bridget Baldwin

with contributions from

Alison Cox, Colin Grigg, Caro Howell and Miquette Roberts

TATE GALLERY PUBLISHING

Cover
Photograph by Nick Turpin featuring Bridget Riley's *Fall* 1963

ISBN 1 85437 236 X (pack)
A catalogue record for this publication is available from the British Library

Published by order of the Tustees of the Tate Gallery
© Tate Gallery 1997 All rights reserved
Published by Tate Gallery Publishing Limited
Millbank, London SW1P 4RG
Designed by Caroline Johnston
Printed in Great Britain by TWP Services Limited, London

Illustration credits
Photographs of works of art by Tate Gallery Photography Department
Photographs on pp.9, 10 by Sarah Weston-Jones
Word-mood picture on p.13 by Colin Grigg
Cartoon on p.40 by Christopher Webster

Copyright credits
Illustration on p.9 shows Naum Gabo's
Head No.2 1916, enlarged version 1964 © Nina Williams 1997
Illustration on p.10 shows Mark Rothko's
Black on Maroon 1958–9 © ARS, NY and DACS, London 1997
p.14 Asger Jorn © The Artist 1997
p.21 Anselm Kiefer © The Artist 1997
p.24 Max Beckmann © VG Bild-Kunst, Bonn 1997

CONTENTS

5 **Using this Pack**

7 **Introduction**
The Tate Gallery at Millbank [7]
First Steps to Looking [10]
Art and Language [11]

16 **Contexts and Themes**
Art and History [16]
Landscape and Nature [20]
Portraits and Identity [23]
Universal Themes [26]

29 **Making and Meaning**
Light and Colour [29]
Abstract Art [31]
Contemporary Art [34]
Materials and Techniques [36]

39 **Planning a Visit**
Making your Booking [39]
Researching Personal Studies [41]
Drawing in the Gallery [44]
More Ideas for the Gallery [46]

48 **Some Vocabulary**

USING THIS PACK

Looking into the Tate has been written for anyone who:

- is planning an educational visit to the Tate Gallery
- has never visited the Tate Gallery before and wants some guidance on how to look purposefully at its collections
- is using the Tate Gallery to research a personal study.

We hope that it will help teachers, community group leaders, students and parents as well as the general visitor.

The Tate's collections are very large and its displays change completely every year, so this pack cannot be like a catalogue. Instead it suggests strategies to look at any work of art and also gives accessible information about some key Tate works. It offers practical advice for planning a visit and ideas for things to do in the Gallery.

IMAGES

All reproductions are in black and white because it is hoped that they will not be used as a substitute for visiting the Gallery. If you wish to order colour reproductions please telephone Tate Gallery Publishing on: **0171 887 8870**

KEEPING THIS PACK UP TO DATE

In the folder you will find a current display guide and some sheets on individual works of art which are likely to be shown in the year you bought the pack. Between March and June of each year the Gallery is completely rehung so that displays are changed entirely, but this does not mean that you will need to buy a new pack. When you need the current *display guide* and *focus sheets* please telephone Tate Education on: **0171 887 8887.**

Looking into the Tate can be kept up to date until May 2000, when the Tate at Millbank will become the Tate Gallery of British Art and the new Tate Gallery of Modern Art will open at Bankside.

CHECK IT IS ON DISPLAY

The works of art cited in this pack may not all be on display at the time of your visit. If you are planning to do your own teaching and you wish to look at particular works it is essential to check that they will be exhibited. Please telephone the Information Office on: **0171 887 8734**

This pack provides lists of works suitable for exploring a range of themes, but it does not have room to include full explanations of them. If you are on a preparation visit, before setting out around the galleries you may ask first at the Information Desk which of your chosen works are on display. Captions by each work provide useful information.

INTRODUCTION

The Tate Gallery at Millbank

The Tate Gallery is one of the world's great art museums, attracting more than two million visitors a year.

HOW OLD IS THE GALLERY?

The Gallery was opened in 1897 by the Prince of Wales. Henry Tate, a wealthy sugar merchant and philanthropist, had offered his collection of modern British art to the nation together with funds to build a gallery. On the site finally chosen for the gallery there was once a holding prison for convicts being shipped to Botany Bay in Australia.

The original Gallery was only one-seventh the present size. The building, designed by Sidney Smith, suggests a neo-roman temple of British art and proclaims the power and cultural confidence of Victorian Britain, whose empire spanned the world. Notice Britannia at the top of the facade accompanied by a lion and a unicorn.

Henry Tate's original gift of sixty-seven works of art included such lasting favourites as Sir John Everett Millais's *Ophelia* and John William Waterhouse's *The Lady of Shallot*.

HOW DID THE TATE DEVELOP?

Initially called the National Gallery of British Art, it in fact fell short of Tate's ideal, as it was under the control of the National Gallery in Trafalgar Square: it was not until 1954 that it finally achieved complete managerial independence. In 1917 the Tate was made responsible for the national collection of British painting of all periods, and also for the national collection of modern art. In 1920 the official title was changed to the National Gallery, Millbank, to reflect these changes in the scope of the Collection. However, Tate's name was so firmly attached to the institution that in 1932 it became officially known as the Tate Gallery.

By 1906 the Gallery had doubled in size and in 1910 the art dealer J.J. Duveen paid for extensions to house the Turner Bequest. Over the years there have been many other developments. In 1987 the Turner Collection was rehoused in the purpose-built Clore Gallery, designed by Sir James Stirling.

In order to make the Collection more accessible to the other parts of the country, the Tate has in recent years created galleries in Liverpool (opened 1988) and St Ives (opened 1993).

WHAT LIES IN THE FUTURE?

The Tate Gallery of Modern Art
In the year 2000 the Tate Gallery of Modern Art will open at Bankside in Southwark, near the Globe Theatre and across the river from St Paul's Cathedral.

The building was originally a power station, designed in 1947 by Sir Giles Gilbert Scott. It has now been completely emptied and redesigned as an enormous art gallery by the Swiss architects Herzog and de Meuron. The new gallery will show the Tate's collection of international modern and contemporary art. British modern art will be represented at both the new and the original sites.

The Tate Gallery of British Art
In the year 2000 the original gallery at Millbank will again become the National Gallery of British Art, presenting art in this country from the Renaissance to the present day.

WHAT IS IN THE TATE COLLECTION?

The Tate Gallery is responsible for collecting British art from about 1550, and international modern art. The Collection centres on painting and sculpture, but there are also substantial numbers of watercolours, drawings and prints. After Henry Tate's gift of his own collection, the key event in the Tate's collecting of British art was the arrival of the Turner Bequest. When Britain's greatest Romantic painter, J.M.W. Turner, died in 1851 he had bequeathed around three hundred oil paintings and a staggering twenty thousand works on paper to the nation, and in 1910 these works were transferred to the Tate Gallery from the National Gallery in Trafalgar Square. Before this, the Tate had been responsible only for modern British art, defined as artists born after 1790 (Turner was born in 1775). In 1917 the Tate was made responsible for earlier British art and modern foreign art.

The Collection now includes:
- over 4,000 paintings
- nearly 1,400 sculptures (including reliefs and installations)
- over 6,000 unique works on paper
- nearly 10,000 prints
- over 500 miscellaneous items (including photography)
- 38,000 works in the Turner Bequest.

WHAT IS ON DISPLAY?

The Tate shows works of art in a number of ways.

New Displays
Even with galleries in London, Liverpool and St Ives, the Tate can only display a small part of its total collection at any one time. In 1989 it was decided to change the displays each year. This programme, called *New Displays*, brings different works on view and reveals new interpretations through thought-provoking juxtapositions of famous and lesser-known paintings and sculpture.

Major Exhibitions
The Gallery provides an exciting, high-quality programme of major loan exhibitions in modern, contemporary and British art. These may include retrospectives of single artists, such as *Bonnard* (1998) and *Pollock* (1999), or themed exhibitions, such as *Rossetti, Burne-Jones and Watts: Symbolism in Britain 1860–1910* (1997) and *Gods and Heroes* (1999).

Details of forthcoming exhibitions are given in the *Tate Exhibitions* leaflet, published three times a year.

Art Now
Established in 1995, this room showcases experimental contemporary art, with the artist often creating works specially for the space.

Special Displays
These are exhibitions drawn mainly from the collection and sometimes supplemented by one or two key loans. They may present a body of works by a single artist, such as *Hogarth the Painter* (1997) or explore a theme such as *Picturing Blackness in British Art* (1996).

The Turner Prize
The Turner Prize aims to honour an outstanding British artist each year and to bring new developments in the visual arts to the attention of a wider audience.

Initiated by the Tate's Patrons of New Art, the exhibition has become the most talked-about event in contemporary art, thanks to the support of Channel 4. An exhibition of the work of the four shortlisted artists takes place each autumn, with the winner announced during a live television broadcast.

Turner Collection Displays
At the top of the Clore Gallery, exhibition rooms show changing displays exploring aspects of Turner's work; these often connect sketches and watercolours with finished oil paintings and prints.

WHAT ARE THE AIMS OF THE TATE?

The central mission of the Gallery is to increase public awareness, understanding and appreciation of the Collection. It achieves this by:
- Presenting the Collection at the Tate Gallery in London, Liverpool and St Ives and through a vigorous programme of loans to museums in this country and abroad.
- Adding to the Collection, for the benefit of this and future generations, through gift, bequest, transfer, purchase or 'acceptance in lieu'.
- Documenting, researching and publishing the Collection, encouraging the development of scholarship within the museum and collaboration with historians and artists outside.
- Caring for the Collection, held in trust for the future, by means of an active programme of conservation and management.
- Arranging a programme of temporary exhibitions to provide a context for the appreciation of the Collection.
- Interpreting the Collection in a way that engages interest, contributes to knowledge and provides education and inspiration for visitors.
- Promoting the Collection to a wide variety of audiences, including new audiences, ranging from the first-time visitor to the scholar.
- Providing research facilities for scholars in the Library, Archive and Works on Paper Study Rooms.

- Collaborating with artists in the presentation, acquisition and documentation of their work, seeking to promote understanding and appreciation of the art of our time, as well as that of the past.

WHY VISIT A GALLERY?

It is very important to understand why a visit to an art gallery to see a work of art is better than looking at the same art in a reproduction:
- You get a sense of size. Some objects can be surprisingly large or small. The impact of a gigantic sculpture or painting can often be very dramatic, and the effect of seeing it in real life rather than as a photograph is something like seeing a film on a big screen rather than on television.
- It is possible to examine a work in great detail, which is often essential to a full understanding. For example, it is useful to see the brushstrokes, chisel marks and other clues as to how the object was made.
- The work of art is displayed in an ideal, well-lit situation, maximising its impact.

- You need to move around sculptures to see them from many sides.
- You can see a work of art alongside other works and make comparisons and contrasts between them. Curators hang works in certain arrangements in order to suggest connections, but visitors will be able to develop meanings for themselves.
- You see frames or other modes of presentation. Frames can make a difference to the way we see a work, and are often designed by the artist to have symbolic or decorative relevance to a painting.
- Much contemporary art is three-dimensional or site-specific, or uses media such as video, light, sound and smell which cannot possibly be experienced through a reproduction.

First Steps to Looking

Visual culture is all around us, influencing what we think and our sense of identity. The many images and artefacts created by artists, designers and the mass media contribute to the particular visual culture that we live in. The Tate Gallery collects and displays only fine art. Traditionally it has shown paintings and sculptures by Western artists, but increasingly it is collecting and showing contemporary work by international artists, including new media such as video.

Art plays a fundamental role in making visible – and challenging – social and personal values and experiences. Art can be used to enrich understanding, for example, of personal relations, of history, of attitudes to nature, of politics and of contemporary society. Learning to look at art makes us more alive to the subtleties, structures and textures of the visual world and helps us to read and deal with its messages.

Many works of art were made in times and places about which we know little and for reasons we cannot easily grasp. However, it is possible to achieve some understanding without a full knowledge of these contexts.

Understanding art is always a combination of supplying meanings from your own cultural interests and knowledge (reading in) and uncovering original meanings (reading out). You can have a fulfilling experience of art no matter where you stand on this spectrum from scholarship to personal interpretation. The approach taken in this pack is a balanced one, providing key facts and themes to help you read out meanings and suggesting strategies for reading in your own.

With younger children and non-specialists it is usually best to begin with personal responses, only introducing relevant external knowledge to test and support their first ideas.

YOU

What is your personal response to a work of art? What do you bring from your personality, your particular experiences and your cultural background?

THE OBJECT

What can you see in front of you? What can you learn from looking closely?

THE SETTING

How does the gallery itself, the way the work is displayed and the other works nearby, frame your view of the work of art? Seen in a different place or in a different way would it mean something else?

THE WORLD

Contextual information about history, art history or the artist's intentions will deepen understanding further.

Art and Language

This section provides ideas to enrich an understanding of visual art and to develop critical and creative language skills.

IT'S GOOD TO TALK!

There is a belief that you should be silent in an art gallery, but it is also a place where people come together to share ideas. Of course, we should all be respectful of the needs of other visitors, but do feel comfortable to talk. Art objects seen at first hand can be a perfect stimulus for talking and writing in imaginative, expressive, objective or critical ways. Bear in mind that some rooms of the Tate Gallery can be busy, so quiet reflective writing may have to wait until after the visit.

DESCRIBING

What is it?
Where is it?
What is it made from?
What scale is it?
What words best describe its shapes/colours/lines /patterns/textures?
What details and symbols can you see?
What do you notice first?
How is the space organised?
Do your eyes travel into an imagined space or do they stay on the surface?
What words best describe its mood or its effect?

FURTHER IDEAS

The repetition game
In groups, take it in turns to name one thing about a work of art. The aim is to be accurate about what you see, without repeating any word. Those who repeat are 'out'. You could adapt the game by insisting on adjectives only or by banning particular words. A 'scribe' may note down the words as a source for subsequent writing.

Unseen images
This activity develops skills of mental imaging and precise description. Describe a work of art for someone who cannot see it, who meanwhile makes a drawing based on what you tell them. How accurate was the description? How was it interpreted? This activity has many variants. In the Gallery it may not be possible to prevent the sketchers from seeing the work described, so instead ask everybody to write or record a description for someone to draw back at home or school.

Or, write a descriptive label to be translated into Braille. This calls for skills of precis and an ability to empathise with the experiences of visually impaired people.

Distances
Describe the different effects of seeing a work from a range of viewpoints. Stand far away from the work, then take six paces in, then move closer. If it is a three-dimensional work stand at the four points of the compass. At each point write a descriptive line.

HYPOTHESISING

How do you think the work of art was made?
What problems did the artist have in making this?
What did the artist do first?
When do you think it was made?
For whom do you think it was made?
What do you think it is communicating?
Why has the artist chosen to use those materials / techniques / devices?
What could it have meant to original viewers?

FURTHER IDEAS

Tried and tested
Divide the group into research teams, giving them a limited time to explain their hypotheses to any of the questions above. They should use their initiative to find supporting information throughout the Gallery. If there are no given answers to hand they must offer reasons for their beliefs.

In the mind of the artist
Imagining you are the artist, write a letter to a fellow artist, explaining how you made the work of art, what difficulties or doubts you experienced and what it means to you.

In the mind of the original viewer
Given that the group has some knowledge of the historical period in which a work of art was made, ask them to write a description and response as if they are viewing it in that era. (Consider the impact of images before our age of visual information overload.)

DEBATING

What did the artist intend to do with this work of art? Does it succeed?
Why do you like it / dislike it?
Should art have a social or moral purpose?
Should art be skillful / realistic / innovative / unique / meaningful / beautiful / difficult?
How realistic is it? How truthful is it?
What does it mean to you?
How and why do your interpretations differ from others?
Does the artist intend you to find your own meanings or is there a 'right answer' to uncover?
Which work in this display is the most important?
Which work should be left in the stores? If you could take one home which would it be?

FURTHER IDEAS

What is art for?
Divide the debating group into traditionalists and modernists, or into aesthetes (art for art's sake) and propagandists (art for social change), no matter what their own inclinations are.

Three views
In groups of three, play the roles of the artist, a supportive patron and a hostile critic discussing a work of art. This could then open out into a group debate.

My view
Write an alternative caption (extended label) for a work of art based on your subjective opinion of it. Think about different kinds of writing about art. When does the writer have to be subjective or objective?

IMAGINING AND FEELING

How does the work of art make you feel?
How do you think the artist felt?
What does it remind you of?
What would it be like if you could smell/touch/
taste/hear it?
If it could speak what would it say?
What sounds or music does it suggest?
What is the oddest thing about it?
Do you see anything hidden or that only you can
see?
Find two works which express opposite feelings.

Word-mood
picture inspired
by Karl Schmidt-
Rottluff's
**Woman with a
Bag** 1915

FURTHER IDEAS

Walk into the frame
Use the following as starting points for
    writing poetry:
Imagine that you have just dived into that
    pool/walked through that window/
    travelled beyond the frame.
Are you alone?
What is the temperature?
What can you hear and smell?
How does your body/skin feel?
What memories do you have?
What colour is the light?
What is the season?
What is the time of day?
Are you indoors or outdoors?
What is this world made from?
What texture is this world?
What are the people like who live here?
You can see something – go over and tell us
    what it is.
Go for a walk beyond the edge – what do you
    see?

Some suggested atmospheric works for this
activity:
• *Murals for the Four Seasons Restaurant, Sea-
  gram Building* 1958–9 Mark Rothko
• *Nocturne in Blue and Gold: Old Battersea Bridge*
  c.1872–5 J.A.M. Whistler
• *Norham Castle, Sunrise* c.1845–50, or many
  others by J.M.W. Turner
• *Sketch for 'Hadleigh Castle'* c.1828–9 John
  Constable

The furniture game
Explore associations.
For example:

If this was furniture it would be a church pew
If this was weather it would be a stiff wind
If this was a drink …
If this was a tree …
If this was …

Word cards
Before the visit, write words on slips of paper
(about four per person), for example,
'bumpy/ice cream/furry/panic'. With each
work of art seen, children can select any of
their words they feel are appropriate, perhaps
explaining their choice. The resulting lateral
surprises can provide interesting insights.

Acrostic poems
Select a work of art sited where groups can sit
without interruption, and with an appropriate
title. For example, a ten year old boy wrote
this about *Adieu* by George Baselitz:
  A man
  Drags himself
  Into another
  Empty
  Universe

Word-mood pictures
Identify words for different passages or aspects
of a work of art. For example, the sea may be
calm but people in a boat may feel *panic*, while
a shark circling may be *excited*. An abstract
image may suggest descriptions of colours or
textures. Map out these words visually, referring to the work of art, using coloured pens or
writing the words in appropriate visual ways,
for example using repetition or marks that are
droopy, shaky, bold, etc.

NARRATIVES

Many works of art in the Tate Gallery are ideal for understanding the structures of stories and how visual images can be organised to communicate them. This can lead to imaginative storytelling, writing and drama work.

STARTING POINTS
- What story is being told?
- How does the story unfold over time?
- What devices in the composition are being used to tell the story? For example, do you read the picture right to left, do your eyes focus on a significant event in the centre, are your eyes led through a window to see a clue?
- As a viewer, where are you made to feel you are positioned? Are you outside, high up, looking through a door?
- Are there any significant or symbolic objects?
- How are figures used to communicate meanings? Look at their poses, facial expressions, gesture, clothes and props.
- How do pictorial elements such as light and colour create the particular mood?
- How much does the artist leave it up to you to create your own story?
- Does it remind you of anything you have seen in a film or on television?

Like stories in a book, these works of art relate to events over a period of time:
- *The Deluge* 1920 Winifred Knights
- *A Hopeless Dawn* 1888 Frank Bramley
- *Past and Present Nos.1, 2* and *3* 1858 Augustus Leopold Egg
- *The Saltonstall Family* 1636–7 David des Granges
- *The Death of Major Peirson, 6 January 1781* 1783 John Singleton Copley
- *The Dance* 1988 Paula Rego
- *The Resurrection, Cookham* 1923–7 Stanley Spencer
- *The Autobiography of an Embryo* 1933–4 Eileen Agar (less literal than the others listed)

These works illustrate scenes in dramatic or expressive ways. They are like frozen moments in time:
- *The Doctor* 1891 Luke Fildes
- *An Avalanche in the Alps* 1803 Philip James de Loutherbourg
- *A Lion Devouring a Horse* 1767 George Stubbs
Some of these frozen moments are from well-known stories in literature:
- *Lady Macbeth Seizing the Daggers* 1812 Henry Fuseli
- *Ophelia* 1851–2 John Everett Millais

In these works of art, symbolic objects help to tell the story:
- *A Hopeless Dawn* 1888 Frank Bramley (e.g. the guttering candle)
- *Past and Present Nos.1, 2* and *3* 1858 Augustus Leopold Egg (e.g. the rotten apple)
- *Beata Beatrix* 1864–70 Dante Gabriel Rossetti (e.g. the opium poppy)
- *Carnival* 1920 Max Beckmann (e.g. the monkey mask)

Some works of art contain features of narratives, but also seem to suggest that many stories could be lying there still to be told.

They can be conveyed in unreal or mysterious ways:
- *Village Myths No.36* 1983 Alan Davie
- *Landscape at Iden* 1929 Paul Nash
- *Bouquet with Flying Lovers* 1934–7 Marc Chagall
- *Carnival* 1920 Max Beckmann

They can be conveyed in the irrational language of dreams:
- *Titania and Bottom* c.1790 Henry Fuseli
- *The Fairy Feller's Master Stroke* 1855–64 Richard Dadd
- *The Reckless Sleeper* 1928 René Magritte
- *The Uncertainty of the Poet* 1913 Giorgio de Chirico

Or they can be conveyed in a child's visual language:
- *Letter to my Son* 1956–7 Asger Jorn
- *Nanny, Small Bears and Bogeymen* 1982 Paula Rego
- *After Us, Liberty* 1949 Constant Nieuwenhuys

Asger Jorn
Letter to my Son
1956–7

FURTHER IDEAS

Stories in time

Investigate how still visual images deal with time in stories. Look at stories told through friezes (e.g. the Bayeux tapestry). Discuss how realism is compromised by including scenes from the past or future. Relate these concepts to the development of film.

Before and after

Hypothesise the before and after of the story shown in the picture, developing from the clues given. Freeze those moments in time and create your own tableaux, referring to the styles and poses in the picture. Unfreeze them and act out a mini-play, giving words to the characters. You could even give voices to animals and inanimate objects.

Make a picture illustrating one of these moments before or after. Try to use similar colours or story-telling devices as in the original work of art.

Looking at works of art which suggest many stories:

Chain story

This works well if the image has many details. Point to one feature. Ask someone to begin the story. Point to another object and ask someone else to continue the story incorporating the new object. And so on.

The way we see it

In small groups create your own story from the picture. Each group can then tell, read or act it out to the others.

Dream story

Write a dream story based on a suitable work of art. For example, *The Reckless Sleeper* by Rene Magritte shows a man dreaming of a blue ribbon, a bird, a candle, an apple and a hat. What story links these unrelated objects?

Storybooks for toddlers

Having looked at a work of art expressed in children's visual language, 'tell' a story in pictures for a child who is too young to read. You could make this in the form of a book.

SPEAKING PICTURES

Works of art can be used to develop empathy for other people and drama skills of speech and characterisation.

Some works show figures in the act or posture of speaking:
- *Man Pointing* 1947 Alberto Giacometti
- *The Health of the Bride* 1889 Stanhope A. Forbes
- *A Scene from 'The Beggar's Opera' VI* 1731 William Hogarth

Some show people in the act of telling stories:
- *A Youth Relating Tales to Ladies* 1870 Simeon Solomon
- *The Boyhood of Raleigh* 1870 John Everett Millais

There are people shown talking in groups:
- *Mr Oldham and his Guests* 1750 Joseph Highmore
- *The Strode Family c.1738* William Hogarth

In other works, people are not speaking but seem to be thinking:
- *The Machine Minders* 1956 Ghisha Koenig
- *A Lady Reading* 1909–11 Gwen John

FURTHER IDEAS

Hotseating

One person plays the character in an artwork, with others asking questions like 'what would you do if …?' 'what's your favourite …?'

Body langugage

Looking at figurative works of art, investigate and act out the different postures of speech, for example, begging, declaiming, grabbing attention, uttering. Think about how figurative artists need to know body language as well as actors do. You could make drawings of these postures.

Create monologues

Imagine the boredom of a sitter for a portrait. If a character is reading a letter or book, what does it say and what are their thoughts? If a character is telling a story or making a speech what are they saying?

Create dialogues

Role play two or more characters having a conversation. Or have a dialogue with a work of art, for example with Magritte's *The Future of Statues*.
[Person playing the viewer: 'What's it like up there with your head in the clouds?'
Person playing the art work: 'It's like flying'
And so on.]
Introduce two characters from different pictures or sculptures to one another.

CONTENTS AND THEMES

Art and History

The Tate Gallery is an excellent resource for understanding history. You can see evidence of styles and social and cultural movements in Britain over the last four hundred and fifty years, and in Europe and the United States in the twentieth century.

A WORD OF WARNING

Art cannot be seen as a straightforward illustration of how people lived in the past. For example, sitters often wear timeless fantasy dress to flatter themselves in their portraits. Art can only provide us with partial glimpses and myths of the past, the complete truth of which will always elude us. Similarly, real-life events are transformed because they are channelled through the conventions of making art and the choices made by the artist (or patron) about what to include, exclude, emphasise or distort.

The poet T.S. Eliot said, 'The past should be altered by the present, as much as the present is altered by the past.' We can only see the past through our own eyes.

THE HISTORY CURRICULUM

Art objects in the Tate Gallery can be used to explore the following National Curriculum topics:

KEY STAGE ONE
- Sea, town and landscapes in the past – how have places changed?
- Changes in childhood and domestic life
NB The Tate's Collections are excellent for these broad themes because it is easy in one visit to make connections across time. Also, much historic British art is accessible in that it is realistic in content rather than mythological or religious.

KEY STAGE TWO
- Life in Tudor times
NB There are usually about a dozen Tudor portraits on display, including one monarch, *Queen Elizabeth I c.1575*, attributed to Nicholas Hilliard.
- Victorian Britain
NB There is an extensive collection of Victorian art whose narrative content make them easily accessible. Be aware, however, that they often deal with sensitive themes such as adultery, prostitution and childhood mortality.

- Britain since 1930
NB The works on display from this period offer evidence of styles and cultural attitudes rather than a straightforward picture of modern life. It also becomes harder to define many modern artists as British by nationality or cultural allegiance. A visit would be most useful if it focused, for instance, on the Second World War or contemporary art, rather than on Britain.

KEY STAGE THREE
- The making of the UK
- Britain 1750–c.1900
- The twentieth century
NB If as a history specialist you feel you have less knowledge of art than you need to maximise a gallery visit, we can arrange a gallery talk by a cultural historian tailored to your needs.

QUESTIONS TO ASK ABOUT ANY WORK

It is not always necessary, or even possible, to know the answers to some of these questions. The process of speculation is important.
- Without looking at the label when do you think it was made? Why do you think that?
- What condition is it in? Does it look precious? Has it been cared for? Was it made to last, so that it could record something for posterity?

- Was it made to be displayed here, or in a stately home, a private room, a public building …?
- Was it made for someone else? In other words, was it commissioned by a patron?
- What was it made for? For propaganda? Was it public or private? Was it made for largely aesthetic reasons, or as a way to display status or to tell a moral story?
- Does it record how people lived or is it obviously contrived to convey a message? In what ways is it realistic or not?
- How was it made? Compared to other works of the same period, is it more advanced? Were the materials and techniques used expensive? Do you think the artist made it alone or with a team?

CROSS-CURRENTS

The following issues cut across historical periods. They can be discussed using any of the suggested works. Remember to check that a particular work is on display.

How have images been used to influence political opinion or loyalty?
- *Queen Elizabeth 1* c.1575 attributed to Nicholas Hilliard
- *Captain Thomas Lee* 1594 Marcus Gheeraerts (Lee is appealing to Elizabeth I)
- *The Field of Waterloo* 1818 J.M.W. Turner
- *The Weeping Woman* 1937 Pablo Picasso (Related to the bombing of Guernica)
- *Cecil Court London WC2 (The Refugees)* 1983–4 R.B. Kitaj

How have the relative roles of men and women been represented and how have they changed?
- *Three Ladies Adorning the Term of Hymen* 1773 Joshua Reynolds (Marriage as woman's destiny)
- *Woman's Mission: Companion of Manhood* 1863 George Elgar Hicks (Dutiful wife supports bereaved husband)
- *A Favourite Custom* 1861 Laurence Alma Tadema (Exotic bathing beauties)
- *Angel of Anarchy* 1936–40 Eileen Agar (This was originally a male head but the artist wrapped feminine textiles round the face to make it androgynous)
- *Unique Forms of Continuity in Space* 1913 Umberto Boccioni (Muscular masculinity forges into the future)

How has domestic life been represented and how has it changed?
- *The Saltonstall Family* 1636–7 David des Granges (Maternal mortality and trussed-up children)
- *Anna Maria Astley, Aged Seven, and her Brother Edward, Aged Five and a Half* 1767 Francis Cotes. (Children allowed to play)
- *Past and Present Nos.1, 2 and 3* 1858 Augustus Leopold Egg (Adultery and family break-up)
- *The Artist's Children* 1915 Augustus John (A liberal father proud of his large brood)
- *Double Nude Portrait: The Artist and his Second Wife* 1937 Stanley Spencer (A focus on the sexual relationship of a couple)

Cultural identity and colonialism – how are non-Western people represented?
- *Colonel Mordaunt's Cock-Match* 1784–6 John Zoffany (Colonials play with Indians)
- *The Death of Major Peirson, 6 January 1781* 1783 John Singleton Copley (The loyal black servant avenges his master's death)
- *The Beloved ('The Bride')* 1865–6 Dante Gabriel Rossetti (A black maid is a foil to a white woman's beauty)

Economics, industrialisation and changing environments
- *The Opening of Waterloo Bridge (Whitehall Stairs, June 18th, 1817)* 1832 John Constable (The changing face of London)
- *The Iron Forge* 1772 Joseph Wright of Derby
- *Abstract Speed – The Car has Passed* 1913 Giacomo Balla
- *The Toy Shop* 1962 Peter Blake (Consumer choice)

A POTTED HISTORY OF ART IN BRITAIN

The Sixteenth Century (1500s)

- The Reformation in the 1530s led to a prohibition of religious images
- Artists were paid by royalty (and increasingly, nobility) to make images reflecting their power and status
- Artists made many other forms of decorative art as well as portraits
- They worked in guilds, at first usually anonymously
- More Flemish artists became famous (e.g. Hans Holbein)
- The court of Elizabeth stimulated much art production
- Portraits tended to be 'iconic' (stiff and decorative, like religious effigies)

SOME WORKS OF ART

- *Captain Thomas Lee* 1594 Marcus Gheeraerts
- *A Man in a Black Cap* 1545 John Bettes
- *Mary Rogers, Lady Harington* 1592 Marcus Gheeraerts
- *An Unknown Lady* 1565–8 Hans Eworth
- *An Allegory of Man* c.1570 Anglo–Flemish School (A rare religious subject)

Marcus Gheeraerts
the Younger
**Captain Thomas
Lee** 1594

The Seventeenth Century (1600s)

- A growth in European trade
- Further influx of Flemish artists (e.g. Anthony Van Dyck) influencing style and content
- Increase in nobility and gentry commissioning portraits, but visual arts continue to centre on the Court
- Portraits became more painterly and alive
- The first landscape paintings in Britain
- Collapse of court patronage during and after the Civil War
- After 1660, a revival of court patronage. A great expansion of painters, for example making still life and landscape

SOME WORKS OF ART

- *Endymion Porter* 1643–5 William Dobson
- *Landscape with Rainbow, Henley-on-Thames* c.1690 Jan Siberechts
- *Cookmaid with Still Life of Vegetables and Fruit* c.1620–5 Sir Nathaniel Bacon
- *Still Life* 1698 Edward Collier

The Eighteenth Century (1700s)

- Britain establishes an Empire
- Wealth and stability extends middle-class patronage
- Landscapes and group portraits grow in popularity
- Hogarth generates own markets by making 'ready to buy' images and expresses his own vision through satire
- Royal Academy established in 1768 – exhibiting club, art college and arbiter of taste
- Joshua Reynolds, President of the Royal Academy, attempts to promote serious 'history' painting with classical and biblical themes, while making a fortune from glamorous portraits in the Grand Manner
- Aritstocrats and artists make Grand Tours of France and Italy

SOME WORKS OF ART

- *O the Roast Beef of Old England (The Gate of Calais)* 1748 William Hogarth
- *Mrs Hartley as a Nymph with a Young Bacchus* 1773 Joshua Reynolds (A portrait dressed up in classical mythology)
- *The Golden Age* 1776 Benjamin West (A proper history painting!)
- *Haymakers* and *Reapers* 1785 George Stubbs (Productive agricultural labour)
- *An Iron Forge* 1772 Joseph Wright of Derby

The Nineteenth Century (1800s)

- Industry and cities grow dramatically
- Artists increasingly express an individual vision (e.g. William Blake)
- Romanticism and awe at the power of nature (e.g. J.M.W. Turner)
- Scientific study of nature for more naturalistic landscapes (e.g. John Constable)
- From 1830s, a concept of art as good for the nation's industry and morals …
- … Leads to growth of museums and art schools
- Subject matter includes industry, urban and working-class life and the heroism of ordinary people
- Royal Academy loses its domineering influence c.1890s
- Dominance of scientific ideologies …
- … Leads to a mass crisis of faith which artists strive to overcome (e.g. the Pre-Raphaelites)
- Aestheticism rejects naturalism and narrative (e.g. J.A.M. Whistler)
- End of century, Sickert and the New English Art Club focus on pictorial elements such as paint texture and colour, influenced by the Impressionists

SOME WORKS OF ART
- *Snow Storm – Steam Boat off a Harbour's Mouth* 1842 J.M.W. Turner
- *Cloud Study* 1822 John Constable
- *Pegwell Bay, Kent – A Recollection of October 5th 1858* 1958–60 William Dyce
- *The Derby Day* 1856–8 William Powell Frith
- *Christ in the House of His Parents ('The Carpenter's Shop')* 1849–50 John Everett Millais
- *Nocturne in Blue and Gold: Old Battersea Bridge* 1872–5 J.A.M. Whistler
- *Boulogne Sands* 1888–91 Philip Wilson Steer

The Twentieth Century (1900s)

- City living and speed, two world wars, increasing global knowledge and communications
- Decline of history and narrative painting
- Individualism, but sometimes working in groups, with a common manifesto (e.g. Vorticism)
- Focus on form rather than content (e.g. Duncan Grant, Ben Nicholson, Henry Moore)
- 1939–51 wartime austerity in art and design
- Expressions of horror, related to experience of Second World War (e.g. Francis Bacon)
- 1951 Festival of Britain provides the British people with a lift of optimism – the modern look (pure, functional and international)
- From mid-1950s American influence led to British Abstraction and Pop art
- Consumer and media culture – images infiltrate every sphere of life
- Nostalgia for a lost Britain and lost spirituality (e.g. John Piper)
- From 1960s growth of 'museum art' – designed specifically to be seen in a gallery and reflecting on the nature of art
- Widening definitions of what constitutes and who makes fine art
- Wider audiences for contemporary art.

SOME WORKS OF ART
- *Merry-Go-Round* 1916 Mark Gertler
- *Painting* 1937 Ben Nicholson
- *Three Studies for Figures at the Base of a Crucifixion* 1944 Francis Bacon
- *$he* 1958–61 Richard Hamilton
- *Break-Off* 1961 Gillian Ayres
- *Slate Circle* 1979 Richard Long
- *Cold Dark Matter: An Exploded View* 1991 Cornelia Parker

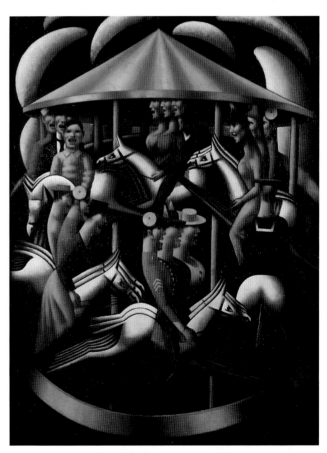

Mark Gertler
Merry-Go-Round
1916

Landscape and Nature

HOW NATURAL IS LANDSCAPE?

The landscape of this planet is so touched by humans that it is now almost artificial and most representations of landscape contain clear evidence of this. Other works of art attempt to preserve or idealise wilderness, offering an idyll that we can no longer experience in reality.

Different views

An artist's representation of the external world, no matter how naturalistic or accurate, will always be conditioned by their own (or their patron's) 'view'. A work of art is always artificial.

Look at a landscape painting. How would the scene change if the artist was one of the following, or how would you describe the scene if you were one of the following?
- a farm labourer
- a land owner
- a property developer
- a tour operator
- a bird watcher

Changes in attitudes to nature taken by artists, patrons and the public are evident in works of art from the seventeenth century to the present day. Early English landscapes, for example, were often celebrations of land ownership and agricultural productivity:
- *A View of The Grove, Highgate* 1696 Jan Siberechts (A 'portrait' of an estate)
- *A Kill at Ashdown Park* 1743 James Seymour (Aristocratic wealth and landownership)

Today artists such as Anselm Kiefer convey strong messages about ecological damage or anxieties about urban life.
- *Lilith* 1987–9 Anselm Kiefer (São Paulo in Brazil appears as a chaotic ruin)

Inside or outside

With the invention of the paint tube in the mid-nineteenth century, oil paint became portable. Before then artists had to make sketches of nature, or use conventions ('the correct way to paint trees'), or the imagination, to provide the information for painting the finished work in the studio. The Impressionists were the first art movement to exploit fully the potential of painting *en plein air* (out of doors), in keeping with their emphasis on painting real life as directly as possible.
- *The Hayfield* 1855–6 Ford Madox Brown (Painted out of doors to capture the effect of twilight)

Look at a landscape painting.
How accurate is the artist's representation?
Can you tell or guess whether it was made out-doors or in the studio?
Is the light natural or enhanced for theatrical effect?
How has the artist adapted or manipulated the view?
How has the artist influenced your reaction?

Truth

The impulse to record our environment 'truthfully' has been a recurring stimulus for artists. Many artists have used empirical methods borrowed from or related to science in order to capture the reality and detail of nature. In the eighteenth century topography (accurate documentation of places) was at its height, and George Stubbs was studying the anatomy of horses to be more true to nature. More recently, to record places artists have used photography and methods borrowed from other professions such as archaeology or surveying.
- *In the Road to Santa Maria de'Monti, near Naples: Morning* 1781 Thomas Jones (Picturesque topography)
- *Mare and Foals in a River Landscape* 1785 George Stubbs
- *Cloud Study* 1822 John Constable
- *Le Bec du Hoc, Grandcamp* 1885 Georges Seurat (Simulating the optical process of seeing colour in strong light)
- *A Hundred Mile Walk* 1971–2 Richard Long (A philosophical and emotional chart of a solitary walk)
- *A Sudden Gust of Wind (After Hokusai)* 1993 Jeff Wall (Capturing a moment on camera)

NATURE AS METAPHOR

The natural world has often been used by artists as a metaphor for human existence. Sometimes this is overtly religious, sometimes a longing for a pagan or primeval past.

- *A Hilly Scene c.1826–28* Samuel Palmer
- *Snow Storm: Hannibal and his Army Crossing the Alps* exh 1812 J.M.W. Turner
- *Our English Coasts ('Strayed Sheep'), 1852* 1852 William Holman Hunt
- *Pegwell Bay, Kent – A Recollection of October 5th 1858* ?1858–60 William Dyce (Aeons of space and time in the fossils, comet and sea contrast with the relative transcience of human lives)
- *Bathers at Moritzburg* 1909/26 Ernst Ludwig Kirchner (Nudists getting back to nature)

Until the seventeenth century it was rare to find a 'pure' landscape – without a narrative, portrait or other focus of interest. However, even where nature takes a back seat, it often has an important metaphorical or subjective role.

- *William Style of Langley* 1636 British School (Symbolism of the tamed garden)
- *Sir Brooke Boothby* 1781 Joseph Wright of Derby (The sitter's interest in Rousseau's philosophy of getting back to nature)

Mother Nature

The classical division of Man as Rational and Cultured versus Woman as Emotional and Natural is present in many works of art. The organic processes of procreation, fertility and the beauty present in the natural world have meant that images of women and nature are frequently paralleled or metaphorically linked.

- *The Cookmaid with Still Life of Vegetables and Fruit c.1620–5* Nathaniel Bacon
- *The Schutz Family and Their Friends on a Terrace* 1725 Philip Mercier (The young bride is led from untamed nature to the civilised terrace where her betrothed sits)
- *Ophelia* 1851–2 John Everett Millais (The poignant contrast of spring flowers and the dead girl. The various plants also carry symbolic associations of love and pain)
- *Recumbent Figure* 1938 Henry Moore

Landscapes of Pleasure

During the eighteenth century people began to travel for pleasure, both within their own country and abroad. English artists such as Turner travelled to Italy to study not only classical and Renaissance art, but also the physical settings themselves. In the nineteenth century mass tourism developed, as did the notion of leisure time. Poets, artists and the public sought contemplation in landscapes of both picturesque and sublime (awe-inspiring) beauty. Throughout the Collection you will find artists responding to the beauty, the splendour or the mystery of the natural world.

- *Childe Harold's Pilgrimage* exh. 1832 J.M.W. Turner (Picturesque idyll combining all the beauties of Italy)
- *Nocturne in Blue and Gold: Old Battersea Bridge c.1872–5* J.A.M. Whistler (An urban structure transformed into moody mystery)
- *Boulogne Sands* 1888–91 Philip Wilson Steer
- *The Snail* 1953 Henri Matisse (Celebrating the geometry of the snail and the vibrancy of the Mediterranean)

Landscapes of Pain

Environments, both specific and imagined, have been used by artists to express personal, social, religious or political pain and destruction: in such works it is the environment itself, rather than any action performed within it, that conveys the artist's response.

- *The Great Day of His Wrath* 1851–3 John Martin. (A cataclysmic image of the Day of Judgement)
- *Sketch for 'Hadleigh Castle' c.1828–9* John Constable (Painted after the artist's wife had died)
- *Totes Meer (Dead Sea)* 1940–1 Paul Nash (An apocalyptic 'seascape' of crashed war planes)
- *Working Model for 'The Unknown Political Prisoner'* 1955–6 Reg Butler (Intended to stand on the border of East and West Berlin)
- *Lilith* 1987–9 Anselm Kiefer (A cityscape of decay and catastrophe)

Anselm Kiefer
Lilith 1987–9

SCULPTURE OF THE ENVIRONMENT

Historically, European sculpture has had as its focus the human figure. However, during the twentieth century sculptors have experimented with different materials often using found objects from the natural world. Or they have produced works that respond to, reflect or were created to be integrated into, the outside world. Other sculptors, such as Bill Woodrow and Tony Cragg create sculpture from discarded consumer items raising ideas about our impact on the environment.

- *Marine Object* 1939 Eileen Agar (An assemblage of ancient pot, horn and shell found in the sea)
- *Figure (Nanjizal)* 1958 Barbara Hepworth (A response to the Cornish landscape)
- *King and Queen* 1952–3 Henry Moore (One version is sited on the English/Scottish border evoking thoughts of sovereignty)
- *Slate Circle* 1979 Richard Long (Slate is mined for use in buildings, but here arranged in an organic shape)
- *Terra Incognita* 1969–84 Lothar Baumgarten (Human debris in a rainforest)
- *Tree of 12 Metres* 1980–2 Giuseppe Penone (Trees stripped to the core and made vulnerable)
- *The End of the Twentieth Century* 1983–5 Joseph Beuys (Related to a project to 'green' the German city of Kassel)
- *Forms without Life* 1991 Damien Hirst (Real shells, where we usually see them, in a shop or museum display cabinet. Not in the sea where they usually exist)

Portraits and Identity

The Tate Gallery offers many opportunities to explore representations of people across time. For example, one can compare a traditional portrait by Anthony Van Dyck with an expressive portrait by Francis Bacon. Not all figurative images are portraits. For example, a figurative artwork is not a portrait when the sitter is an anonymous model 'acting' as part of a visual story or to communicate an idea, nor is it a portrait when the figure is produced from imagination. A portrait generally exists to communicate messages about a real person, and we very often know who the sitter is. This section deals mainly with portraits, and suggests ways to explore the theme of 'identity'.

QUESTIONS TO ASK ABOUT ANY PORTRAIT

Who may have asked for this portrait to be made?
Who may have decided how the sitter is dressed and posed?
What do the pose, costume, setting and other objects say to you about the sitter?
Where might the portrait have been displayed originally?
Do you think this person was pleased with their portrait?
Was this made for a special occasion?
In what ways is this work realistic or not?
What do the colours, application of paint, scale and frame add to the effect?

PORTRAITS OF THE PAST

Why were they made?
Before photography was invented a painted or sculpted portrait was the only way to record a person's appearance and identity. Portraits were commissioned by wealthy people for a variety of reasons.
- *The Cholmondeley Ladies* c.1600–10 British School (To celebrate an important event such as birth or marriage)
- *Queen Elizabeth I* c.1575, attributed to Nicholas Hilliard (To publicise an important figurehead and to show power and wealth. Public figures often develop a set image which is repeated and is easily recognisable)
- *William Style of Langley* 1636, British School (To tell us about beliefs and allegiances)
- *Giovanna Baccelli* 1782, Thomas Gainsborough (A private portrait of the patron's mistress)
- *Three Ladies Adorning the Term of Hymen* 1773 Joshua Reynolds (To promote a woman ripe for marriage)

Were they made to last?
Yes. One key aim was to preserve the 'likeness' of the sitter beyond death. As a comparison you may find some modern art which is not so physically enduring. For example, Mark Quinn made a cast of his head with his own frozen blood. (*Blood Head*, not owned by the Tate.)

Where were they originally displayed?
They were often made for display in large houses and palaces. People who commissioned or bought lots of art sometimes built 'long galleries' in their houses. Bear in mind that portraits were only one small part of artistic production. The houses of the rich were full of tapestries and furniture and from the eighteenth century, with works of art collected on Grand Tours of Italy and France.

What do the sitters' clothes say about them?
Most of the clothes in these portraits were extremely expensive, especially those from the sixteenth and seventeenth centuries, so they communicate the sitter's wealth and fashionable taste. In the eighteenth century sitters sometimes wore plain robes as these would not date embarrassingly over time. Clothes can also tell you about the sitter's identity. For example, in *Portrait of Mary Rogers, Lady Harington* 1592 by Marcus Gheeraerts, the pattern on the dress relates to the family emblem of a knot, seen in her hand. Clothes also communicate gender roles and occupations. Women's clothes tended to be impractical and decorative, whereas men are seen in the garb of power and profession.

- *Benjamin Hoadly, Bishop of Winchester* 1741 William Hogarth (What does his wig say about him?)
- *Endymion Porter* 1643–5 William Dobson (The rich draped cloak gives the effect of swagger and size)
- *Giovanna Baccelli* 1782 Thomas Gainsborough (The sitter was a professional dancer)

Are there any portraits of people who weren't rich?

Sometimes, artists painted people close to them, such as their family, friends or servants. These tend to be small, private studies.

- *Heads of Six of Hogarth's Servants* 1750–5 William Hogarth

PORTRAITS IN THE TWENTIETH CENTURY

The role of portraiture has changed. Since the invention of the camera it is no longer necessary to paint or sculpt to record appearances for posterity. Social changes have made artists and patrons less interested in displaying status. Artists continued to make traditional portraits because they were considered by some patrons to be more special, flattering or permanent than photographs. However, most twentieth-century portraits in the Tate Gallery have been collected for their innovative qualities or because the artists have delved deeper than surface appearances. Artists have been freed from the demands of patronage and have tended to concentrate on self-expression.

A focus on form and colour

In many portraits of the first half of this century, formal elements (light, colour, arrangements of shapes) became more important than a sitter's features. Sometimes, the artist has used a friend or relative as a model in a painterly exercise.

- *Mrs Mounter at the Breakfast Table* 1917 Harold Gilman
- *Head of a Woman (Fernande)* 1909 Pablo Picasso
- *Mrs St John Hutchinson* 1915 Vanessa Bell

Max Beckmann
Carnival 1920

Expression

Since the eighteenth century we have become more interested in defining ourselves as 'affective' individuals – people with feelings and relationships. The Norwegian Expressionist Edvard Munch said 'No longer should you paint interiors with men reading and women sitting. There must be living beings who breathe and feel and love and suffer.' Modern portraits often focus on intense emotions basic to humanity rather than external features.

- *Dr Rosa Schapire* 1919 Karl Schmidt-Rottluff
- *Carnival* 1920 Max Beckmann (A political allegory, but the figures are also portraits of the artist himself, a friend and Beckmann's dealer)

Decay and distortion

Post-war existentialist philosophies have influenced modern representations of people. In this view of the world, we are no longer seen to possess intact, unchanging identities or bodies. We are not driven by an internal personality (essence) but continually remade by relationships with others and places (existence). In this process we are entirely alone. Certain artists have been obsessed by the realisation of our vulnerability:

- *Study for Portrait II (after the Life Mask of William Blake)* 1955 Francis Bacon
- *Jean Genet* 1955 Alberto Giacometti

The end of flattery

With the declining tradition of grand society portraiture, artists were freed from flattering the sitter. In the post-war era this was combined with an unease about heroism and glory and a realisation of human fallibility.

- *Naked Portrait* 1972–3 Lucian Freud
- *Double Nude Portrait: The Artist and his Second Wife* 1937 Stanley Spencer

Portraiture becomes political

The act of representing others has become increasingly politicised in the twentieth century. An artist's portrayal of an individual's gender, racial origins, social status, sexual orientation, role and interests are now open to fierce debate. Many artists make political statements in their work in the belief that art can act as a catalyst for social change.

- *Missionary Position II* 1985 Sonia Boyce

SELF-PORTRAITS

Why were self-portraits made by artists, who were usually paid to make portraits for others? Well, self-portraits were used to show off status, beliefs or profession and if you had the skill to make such an expensive commodity, then why not make one for yourself? It is a perfect marketing tool.

As we have seen, artists in the twentieth century have been interested in self-exploration. For source material they often use the people closest to hand, that they know best, so it is even more convenient to use oneself.

Do you think self-portraits tell us more about the artist's true self than a portrait by another artist could? Or do you think perhaps self-portraits can mask or distort in a more calculated and effective way?

What were these artists like as people? Did they like themselves? Were they comfortable looking themselves in the eye? Try it yourself. Do you feel as if you are staring at a strange object or another person?

- *Self-Portrait when Young 1753–58* Joshua Reynolds
- *The Painter and his Pug 1745* William Hogarth
- *Self-Portrait 1902* Gwen John
- *Self-Portrait 1959* Sir Stanley Spencer
- *Self-Portrait with Badges 1961* Peter Blake
- *Untitled 1982* Cindy Sherman

STEREOTYPES AND SYMBOLS

How is identity communicated visually? A sense of identity is shaped by such things as our relationships to other people and the shared experiences we have together. It is formed by the community, time and place that we belong to, by our gender, by our social role and status, and by the way we choose to present ourselves to the world. Some of these things remain constant throughout our lives; others change. Stereotypes and symbols are drawn from these factors and are often used to show a person's characteristics or their position within a social structure. They have a common currency – we all understand them within our own culture – and they are often visual, so they are very useful for artists. However they do not always cross cultural or historical boundaries so they need explaining to people who are unfamiliar with them. For example:

- *Beata Beatrix c.*1864–70 Dante Gabriel Rossetti (A 'portrait' of Rossetti's wife Lizzie Siddall. The radiant bird is the messenger of death; the opium poppy refers to her death from a laudanum overdose; her green dress suggests fertility and life.)

Modern art is usually less rigid in its meanings than Tudor or Victorian portraits:

- *Man with a Thistle (Self-Portrait) 1946* Lucian Freud (Do you think the thistle is symbolic? If the meaning of this picture is for you to decide, what might the thistle communicate about Freud?)

FURTHER IDEAS

Preparing for the visit
When have you posed for a formal photograph? How have you felt when someone has 'snapped' you when you weren't expecting it?

Look at portraits of royalty, rich people and pop stars in magazines like *Hello* or *Smash Hits*. Imagine the conversation between the photographer and the 'sitter' about how they should appear.

Would you want to assume a role in your own portrait?
Would you want to be someone from history or from the present day?
If you take on a role in a portrait how does it make you feel?

Think of someone you know really well – is there something they always wear or carry that makes you think of them? Discuss symbols which are personal, like your own choice of tattoo, compared to symbols that identify you with a group or community, such as a blazer badge.

On a sheet divided into four boxes, list words to describe the self that you think is seen by your teacher, your best friend, a parent, and then how you see yourself. This can be used for discussion, creative writing, or as a stimulus for painting self-portraits.

What would you prefer for your portrait: a sculpted bust; a photograph; a video recording; a painting; or something else?

Following the visit
Each person make or find a plain box. Using a wide range of media – scrap objects, collage, paint, etc. – decorate or add to the boxes to create metaphors for the private and public aspects of self, where the images on the outside show you as the 'public' person seen by others, while the inside of the box is 'private' person seen only by yourself.

Paint a self-portrait which does not show a likeness of your face.

Imagine you are a television celebrity or a pop star. Make a publicity image – using a medium appropriate for reproduction.

Universal Themes

On the whole, The Tate Gallery's collection reflects European cultural interests. However, there is great potential for 'reading out' personal meanings and exploring issues of cross-cultural relevance. This section presents three universal themes, suggesting ways of using works of art to debate such issues.

FAMILY AND LOVE

Objects of desire
How do cultural attitudes differ regarding representations of allure, sex or nudity?
How is the body adorned or concealed to express messages of sexual status?
- *Nude Woman in a Red Armchair* 1932 Pablo Picasso (The artist's young girlfriend)
- *Giovanna Baccelli* 1782 Thomas Gainsborough (The patron's mistress)
- *Double Nude Portrait: The Artist and his Second Wife* 1936 Stanley Spencer
- *King Cophetua and the Beggar Maid* 1884 Edward Burne-Jones (Love across classes)

Homosexual love
- *The Third Love Painting* 1960 David Hockney

Marriage
What colours, clothes and rituals are associated with marriage in different cultures?
- *The Schutz Family and their Friends on a Terrace* 1725 Philip Mercier (A girl is led into the civilising sphere of marriage, perhaps entering the home of a new family)
- *The Health of the Bride* 1889 Stanhope Alexander Forbes (Choosing passion or stability – the sailor may be her first love)
- *Three Ladies Adorning a Term of Hymen* 1773 Joshua Reynolds (Marriage as women's only destiny)
- *The Wedding* 1989–93 R.B. Kitaj (The artist's Jewish wedding)
- *Bride* 1994 Paula Rego (Dressing up and playing role of bride)

Motherhood
- *Three Forms* 1935 Barbara Hepworth (Symbolic of the artist's triplets)
- *The Cholmondeley Ladies* c.1600–10 British School (Swaddled babies)

- *Mrs Johnston and her Son c.*1775–80 George Romney (Tenderness)

Happy Families
- *The Iron Forge* 1772 Joseph Wright of Derby
- *The Bradshaw Family* exh. 1769 Johan Zoffany
- *Sunday* 1985–9 John Lessore

Loss and tragedy
- *Woman's Mission: Companion of Manhood* 1863 George Elgar Hicks (Mourning and woman's role as comforter)
- *Past and Present, Nos.1–3* 1858 Augustus Leopold Egg (Adultery and family collapse)
- *Ophelia* 1894 John Everett Millais (Suicide after lover murdered father)
- *The Kiss* 1901–4 Auguste Rodin (Paolo Malatesta and Francesca da Rimini's forbidden love)
- *Ennui c.*1914 Walter Sickert (Marital boredom)
- *The First Cloud* 1887 William Quiller Orchardson (Arguments and separation)

The cycle of life
- *The Saltonstall Family c.*1636–7 David des Granges
- *The Dance* 1988 Paula Rego (The artist at different life stages, dancing with husband and family. Explores the role of dance in courtship, rites of passage and religion, e.g. Krishna dancing with milkmaids)
- *The Nantes Triptych* 1992 Bill Viola (The moment of birth, the slow fall of man and the death of the artist's mother)

RELIGION: CONNECTING WITH CHRISTIANITY

Religious teaching
How are images used to teach religious knowledge, to instil fear and moral values or to inspire passion? How much do artists try to illustrate religious texts authentically or present personal interpretations?
- *Christ in the House of His Parents ('The Carpenter's Shop')* 1849–50 Sir John Everett Millais
- *Satan, Sin and Death (A Scene from Milton's 'Paradise Lost')* c.1735–40 William Hogarth
- *The Plains of Heaven* 1851–3 John Martin
- *Crucifixion* 1946 Graham Sutherland

Personal visions

How does the private way of seeing relate to the conventional or social vision?

- *The Vision of Eliphaz* and many others by William Blake (A very individual vision mixing the Bible with other myths. How much are religions fertilised across cultures and adapted by individuals?)
- *The Resurrection, Cookham* 1923–7 Stanley Spencer (Artist, wife and friends are resurrected in his village churchyard. How are strange myths or abstract concepts put in familiar settings to become more resonant or tangible?)
- *The Angel of the Flowing Light* 1968 Cecil Collins (Spiritual symbolism of light. Discuss angelic figures in other religions.)

Where are the Tate Virgins?

After the Reformation in the 1530s, religious images were banned in England, although some were still made. It can be argued that the result of this prohibition was a national artistic habit of oblique references to Christian iconography for secular subjects.

- *Queen Elizabeth I c.1575* attributed to Nicholas Hilliard (The alternative Virgin Mary)
- *The Iron Forge* 1772 Joseph Wright of Derby (The format of a nativity)
- *The Death of Major Peirson, 6 January 1781* 1783 John Singleton Copley (The descent from the Cross)

How do religious and secular themes combine in images from other cultures?

Meditation and abstraction

Religious art in many cultures is non-representational. For example, Moslems do not believe that they should attempt to rival God as creators, and so limit their art to geometrical patterns.
Abstraction allows for an expansion of spiritual thought towards sublimity.

- *Murals for the Seagram Building* 1958–9 Mark Rothko (A room for meditation)
- *Zim Zum* Barnett Newman (The creation myth – forms split in two)
- *The Enclosure of Sanctity* 1992–3 Shirazeh Houshiary (Sufi mysticism – sacred geometry)
- *As if to Celebrate I Discovered a Mountain Blooming with Red Flowers* 1981 Anish Kapoor (Organic forms covered in bright pigment – suggests Hindu rituals)

Pantheism and nature worship

- *As if to Celebrate I Discovered a Mountain Blooming with Red Flowers* 1981 Anish Kapoor (As above)
- *A Hilly Scene* 1826–8 Samuel Palmer (Although a Christian church, the spirit resides in rural nature)
- *Laughter Uluru (Ayers Rock) The Cathedral I* 1985 Michael Andrews (Rock sacred to Aborigines)
- *Untitled* 1982–3 Georg Baselitz (Elemental forces – influenced by African sculpture)

WAR AND DEATH

The horrors of war

How are the inexpressible horrors of war contained in images to help us face the thought that they happened? In the twentieth century artists have made us reflect on our actions and on the suffering of individuals. Has this been the artist's role in other cultures and times?

- *Merry-Go-Round* 1916 Mark Gertler (Painted after the artist saw wounded soldiers at a funfair)
- *Three Studies for Figures at the Base of a Crucifixion c.1944* Francis Bacon
- *Weeping Woman* 1937 Pablo Picasso (Painted after the bombing of Guernica)
- *Pink and Green Sleepers* 1941 Henry Moore (In the Underground during the Blitz)
- *Large Tragic Head* 1942 Jean Fautrier (Expressing torture cries heard while hiding from Nazis)
- *Totes Meer (Dead Sea)* 1940–1 Paul Nash (Crashed planes – Nash was an official war artist)

Idealising war

How is war glamorised in images in order to make it seem an acceptable and exciting practice? How are warriors built up as supermen?

- *Unique Forms of Continuity in Space* 1913 Umberto Boccioni (Macho power and speed)
- *Whaam!* 1963 Roy Lichtenstein (Ironic borrowing from a comic)

Childhood mortality

- *The Artist Attending the Mourning of a Young Girl c.1847* John Everett Millais
- *The Doctor* exh. 1891 Luke Fildes
- *The Sick Child* 1907 Edvard Munch

Preserving memories of the lost

Most cultures use visual images in rituals to deal with the reality of death and the grief of losing loved ones, for example Ancient Egyptian burials and the Mexican Day of the Dead.

- *The Saltonstall Family c.1636–7* David des Granges (Dead first wife)
- *The Death of Major Peirson, 6 January 1781 1783* John Singleton Copley
- *Chatterton 1856* Henry Wallis (A young suicidal poet – true story)
- *Beata Beatrix 1864–70* Dante Gabriel Rossetti (Rossetti's wife Lizzie Siddal died of an opium overdose)
- *The Reserve of Dead Swiss 1990* Christian Boltanski

Leaving home

- *Cecil Court, London WC2 (The Refugees) 1983–4* R.B. Kitaj (Jewish refugees. Why are people forced from their homelands? Does any home really belong to us?)
- *The Emigrant's Last Sight of Home 1858* Richard Redgrave (What is it like to emigrate?)
- *The Deluge 1920* Winifred Knights (Explores experiences and cultural myths of flood and natural disaster)

Survival

- *Storm Man 1947–8* Germaine Richier (A monument to man's post-war survival, albeit damaged).
- *Untitled (Vitrine) 1983* Joseph Beuys (Felt, fat, razors, etc. in glass cases. Refers to Beuys being saved from death by these items when stranded after a plane crash. Compare to artefacts for survival in museums)
- *Death Hope Life Fear 1984* Gilbert and George (The survival of the gay way of life)

MAKING AND MEANING

Light and Colour

This section explores how artists' uses of light and colour communicate moods and meanings. Light makes things visible. We can only see objects and colours when there is light. Light and colour, are thus inextricably linked. We react instinctively to dark and bright colours in painting just as we do in life. Since we tend to be fearful of the dark, a predominantly grey painting may make us feel anxious or depressed. Because bright sunshine warms us, so do vivid reds and oranges. Artists can choose to match mood to colour or to surprise us by creating different feelings from those expected of the colours.

Our interpretations of light and colour may be shared universally or culturally, others may be very individual. An artist's use of colour is conditioned not only by choice but by many factors such as peculiarities of the eyes, limited access to pigments, working in a dimly lit studio or out of doors.

PAINTING PLACES

Sunshine and bright colour

The Pre-Raphaelites, the French Impressionists and Fauve painters drew attention to the brilliance of colour in nature, particularly in sunshine, often believing that artists should paint outdoors.

- *Our English Coasts, 1852 ('Strayed Sheep')* 1852 William Holman Hunt
- *Boulogne Sands* 1888–91 Philip Wilson Steer (An example of English Impressionism)
- *André Derain* 1905 Henri Matisse (Painted in the heat of the sun)
- *The Snail* 1953 Henri Matisse (Speaks with the hot colours of the South of France)

How do these sunny paintings make you feel?

Absence of light

Some older paintings in the Tate Gallery can seem to us very dark. This may be due to a lack of artificial light in the place represented, to the often sunless British climate or to the use of subtle natural pigments. Alternatively, and especially since artists have had more choice of colour, the reduction of colour and light may be deliberate to create a mood. A grey day can create absence of hope. The very title of Joseph Farquharson's *The Joyless Winter Day* (1883) makes this plain.

- *Miss Cicely Alexander: Harmony in Grey and Green* 1872 J.A.M. Whistler (A palette of wintery colours)
- *Winter 1956, Yorkshire* 1956 Terry Frost (Colour and texture create a visual equivalent of the experience of sledging. Crisp cool colours are matched by zipping verticals)

SYMBOLISM

Light and dark can be used symbolically to contrast life and death, hope and despair. In such cases it has a dramatic function and can make us focus on what is important in a work and help us to interpret it.

- *An Iron Forge* 1772 Joseph Wright of Derby (Light emanating from a water-powered hammer symbolises optimism at industrial progress)
- *Norham Castle, Sunrise* c.1845–50 J.M.W. Turner (Turner often placed the sun at the centre of his canvases, showing his belief in the sun as god)
- *A Hopeless Dawn* 1888 Frank Bramley (The dawn light over the sea pinpoints the site of tragedy. The guttering candlelight and darkness symbolises the triumph of death)
- *The Doctor* 1891 and *Applicants for Admission to a Casual Ward* 1908 Luke Fildes (The alternation of dark shadows and light echoes the struggle of hope and despair)

PURE COLOUR

In most of the examples given so far, light and colour have been harnessed together. In the twentieth century some artists have considered colour apart from what it represents. If grass is painted red, for example, we are forced to consider afresh the artist's choice and use of colour.

- *Nude, Fitzroy Street, No.1* 1916 Matthew Smith (A nude is usually in soft pinks but here harsh colour is used for its emotional rather than descriptive power)
- *Windows Open Simultaneously (First Part, Third Motif)* 1912 Robert Delaunay (The Eiffel Tower is seen through a pattern of prismatic colours reflected onto the window glass)
- *Composition with Red, Yellow and Blue c.1937–42* Piet Mondrian (Mondrian uses primary colours as building blocks, with a scaffolding of black lines, to create an art of balance)
- *Swinging* 1925 Wassily Kandinsky (Kandinsky wanted to orchestrate colours and lines as a composer would musical notes)
- *Horizontal Stripe Painting: November 1957–January 1958* Patrick Heron (Heron evokes the colours of a sunset sky while creating a sense of fluctuating space by the juxtaposition of warm and cooler tones)

LIGHT AND COLOUR IN SCULPTURE

Light plays a vital function in helping us to 'read' sculpture by helping to model it in the round and by creating a sense of drama. Much sculpture has the colour of its material whether it be wood, bronze or marble. Barbara Hepworth's carved *Torso* 1928, for instance, is guided by the qualities of the stone, its colour and grain. 'Truth to Material' was an important concept from the 1920s. At the same time it focuses attention on the intrinsic qualities of the material. Some materials, such as white marble are light and seem to attract light. White figure sculpture can also refer back to classical sources.

See how the subject matter of selected works relates to the material used. How many classical nudes are bronze when depicting the male, white when portraying the 'pure', delicate female?

The use of colour added to surface has roots in antiquity. In the 1960s, metal sculptures by Anthony Caro and his followers were painted in brightly coloured enamel paints and coloured perspex was also used. More recently, Anish Kapoor has used surfaces of vivid pigments to contrast with stone.

Select a piece of sculpture.
What is its material?
How does the colour affect the way we feel about it?

QUESTIONS TO ASK ABOUT ANY WORK OF ART

Is the colour natural?
Has it been exaggerated?
Has it been reduced or simplified?
Are the colours predominantly warm or cold? A mixture of both?
Have they been used to create a psychological or dramatic impact?
Are they primarily decorative?
Why has the artist selected this range of colours?
What impact does it have on you?

FURTHER IDEAS

Compare two paintings of similar emotional subject matter but with very different colours. Whose choice of colours suits your taste and your perception of that mood? What colours would you choose to paint: Despair? Elation? Tranquility? Panic?

Use *The Snail* 1953 by Matisse to point out primary and secondary colours, to show how complementary colours enhance one another and to see how colours are also weights within a composition. The black is balanced by the heavy red, for example. Hold up your hand so that you conceal the black shape. You can see how it functions to keep the other colours bright.

Abstract Art

INTRODUCTION

Ideas and concepts related to 'abstraction' in art can be explored in a variety of ways. Even works of art which appear highly realistic can be a useful resource in this.

What do we mean by 'abstract'?

The term 'abstract' is generally applied to art which does not present us with recognisable objects but with arrangements of lines, shape and colour. Such art works may relate to the expression of an emotion or idea, attempt to evoke the atmosphere of a particular experience or have symbolic importance, as in much religious art. In Western art history, the term is often used to categorise a vast range of modern works produced from around 1910 onwards. However, for much of human history, art has been based on abstract forms – in Celtic, Mexican, African and Asian art, for example.

Some works of art combine abstract and representational elements.

- *Cossacks* 1910–11 Wassily Kandinsky (This may appear to be a random composition of shapes and colours, but it does use figures and objects to suggest a story of war and the apocalypse. On the right are three Cossacks with long lances. There are also two soldiers on fighting horses, a city on a hill, birds and a rainbow. Do you respond to it differently when you recognise these objects?)
- *Leaves and Shell* 1927 Fernand Léger
- *Abstract Speed – the Car Has Passed* 1913 Giacomo Balla
- *Clarinet and Bottle of Rum on a Mantelpiece* 1911 Georges Braque
- *Bicentric Form* 1949 Barbara Hepworth
- *The Mud Bath* 1914 David Bomberg
- *Equivalents for the Megaliths* 1935 Paul Nash

We can see abstract qualities in all works of art. How?

A realistic painting of a tree, for example, is nothing like a life-size, three-dimensional living tree. It is a composition of lines, colours and shapes arranged by the artist in a particular way to create the illusion of a tree. It is therefore possible to analyse the visual elements of works of art – even those which are not inherently abstract – in this way. *The Saltonstall Family c.1636–7* by David des Granges, for example, has strong abstract properties. It shows

David des Granges
The Saltonstall Family *c.*1636–7

Sir Richard Saltonstall proudly presenting his children from his two marriages. Look at how the figures have been arranged. From the children on Sir Richard's left to the baby on his right, a distinct triangle can be perceived in the composition. Sir Richard of course, appears at the apex of the triangle, emphasising his status within the family. The striking contrast between the darkness of his clothing and the rich reds and pearly whites that surround him is another abstract quality that underscores his importance.

THEMATIC APPROACHES

Pattern and Shape

It is possible to understand the meanings and structures of art by identifying and analysing basic shapes. These might be strikingly obvious or integrated into the composition. Look out for, or make sketches of, regular and irregular shapes, organic and inorganic shapes, symmetry, asymmetry, balance and so on.

- *The Cholmondeley Ladies c.1600–10* British School (How does pattern and shape reinforce the fact that these women are related?)
- *Model for Rotating Fountain* 1925, reassembled 1986 Naum Gabo
- *Swinging* 1925 Wassily Kandinsky (How do these shapes and their arrangement create a sense of movement?)

Compare *Swinging* with:
- *White Relief* 1935 Ben Nicholson
- *Equivalent VIII* 1966 Carl Andre (Andre chose 120 firebricks to work with. This gave him the opportunity to work with many combinations. This is sculpture number eight. What might the other seven have looked like?)
- *Weeping Woman* 1937 Pablo Picasso (Describe the main shapes that make up this woman's face. How do they contribute to the emotional impact of the work?)
- *Marilyn Diptych* 1962 Andy Warhol (Are these serial images of Marilyn Monroe all the same? Which is the 'real' Marilyn? Why does her image fade from left to right?)

Art and Music
Artists have often felt a close relationship between art and music. Whistler, for example, believed that painting was an arrangement of abstract qualities, just as music is an arrangement of abstract sounds that do not imitate sounds in the everyday world. He did not believe that art should have a story-telling purpose.
- *Nocturne in Blue and Gold: Old Battersea Bridge* 1872–5 J.A.M. Whistler

Kandinsky believed that music had the greatest capacity to communicate emotions in a direct way because, unlike literature or much painting, it did not rely on words or on subject matter which required prior knowledge. He had a clinical condition called 'synaesthesia' which meant that he 'heard' colours and shapes as emotional sounds and vice versa. His paintings are expressions of this personal visual language of correspondences.
- *Swinging* 1925 Wassily Kandinsky (How do you interpret his colours and shapes? Can you read his language?)

FURTHER IDEAS

Try listening to a piece of music and make pictures of what it suggests using different colours and different kinds of marks (thin, fat, long, short, repeated patterns, fast lines, slow lines, curvy, angular, etc).

Try making equivalents in painting for musical terms such as rhythm, melody, clash, loud, soft, harmony, disharmony, etc.

Colour and Mood
Many abstract artists use the power of colour to evoke mood. Because these artists do not use obvious storytelling devices, colour is a very important communicator. Try contrasting two abstract works in which shape and colour are used in very different ways. Alternatively look at a work bursting with colour and then one in which there is an absence of colour.

- *Weeping Woman* 1937 Pablo Picasso (What would the effect of this painting be if Picasso had used pastel colours?)
Compare this with:
- *White Relief* 1935 Ben Nicholson

- Compare *Murals for The Seagram Building* 1958–9 Mark Rothko with
- *The Snail* 1953 Henri Matisse

Compare the creamy marble carving
- *Three Forms* 1935 Barbara Hepworth with the gleaming bronze
- *Maiastra* 1912 Constantin Brancusi

- *Norham Castle, Sunrise* c.1845–50 J.M.W. Turner. Compare the colours of this work with others by Turner.

Mark and Gesture
The way that artists apply their chosen media is often a vital clue to the meaning of their work. Look for works which are very expressive. These often trace very clearly the movement of the brush or hand. How would the artist have moved while painting? What would the experience be like?
- *Number 14* 1945 Jackson Pollock
- *Adam* 1951–2 Barnet Newman
- *The Busy Life* 1953 Jean Dubuffet
- *Thermal* 1960 Peter Lanyon
- *Anthony and Cleopatra* 1982 Gillian Ayres
Contrast this with works in which you are hardly aware of the movement of the brush or tool:
- *Hyena Stomp* 1962 Frank Stella
- *Broadway* 1958 Ellsworth Kelly
- *Composition with Grey, Red, Yellow and Blue* 1920–6 Piet Mondrian

---

FURTHER IDEAS

Take a large sheet of paper and take turns to make abstract marks on it. Try 'replying' to each other using marks which evoke similar of different moods. How does your 'conversation' develop?

Size and Scale

Our experience of art works is greatly affected by their size. When you look at a work can your eyes 'take it in' at first glance? Do you have to stand back? What is the impact of a large work? How do you feel when looking at a small work? Can other people look at it with you? Abstract artists often create impact or intimacy in the same ways as representational artists, exploiting scale and other formal devices.

- *Murals for the Seagram Building* 1958–9 Mark Rothko (Here the artist has created a complete room around you. The canvases and their window-like forms are large. What kind of atmosphere does the room create? Is it similar to religious chapels surrounded by paintings?)
- *Snow Storm: Hannibal and his Army Crossing the Alps* 1812 J.M.W. Turner (This is a large picture, the impact of which is intensified by the scale of the tiny figures overwhelmed by a terrible storm)
- *The Snail* 1953 Henry Matisse (A snail, tiny in nature, appears as a giant)
- *Head No.2* 1964 Naum Gabo
- *Whaam!* 1963 Roy Lichtenstein (How would your experience of this work differ if you had seen it in a comic?)

ABSTRACT ART FOR CHANGE

Some may say that abstract art has no meaning or function. It is true that some abstract artists paint because they have an urge to manipulate colour and form for its own sake, and even, like Gary Hume (shortlisted for the Turner Prize in 1996), admit that they just want to make decorative surfaces. Nonetheless, even if the artist intends no meaning, arrangements of form and colour can convey emotions meaningfully to the viewer.

Many abstract artists though *have* intended meanings or have believed in the relevance of abstract art to the modern world. They wanted to create new, exciting forms to change their environment and the way people think.

Kandinsky wanted to communicate universal emotions in a direct way, in that abstraction did not rely on viewers being able to 'read' subject matter.

The Italian Futurist artists Boccioni, Balla and Severini expressed exhilaration at the new world of advanced technology and fast machines.

- *Abstract Speed – the Car Has Passed* 1913 Giacomo Balla

The Constructivist artists called themselves 'artist-engineers' and wanted their work to contribute to the reshaping of modern technological society following the upheaval of the Russian Revolution 1917 and the First World War. Naum Gabo, for example, used modern industrial materials such as plastic, glass and steel to construct his sculptures.

- *Construction in Space (Crystal)* 1937–9 Naum Gabo

Mondrian and Theo van Doesburg worked together from 1917 to1931 as part of the De Stijl ('Style') group. They advocated the use of basic forms such as cubes, verticals and horizontals not just in fine art but also in design to make our environment more harmonious and spiritual.

ABSTRACT ART TODAY

The development of abstraction is usually associated with Modernism in the early twentieth century. However artists continue to use and explore abstraction in various experimental ways.

- *Abstract Painting* 1990 Gerhard Richter (The paint is applied with long plastic batons dragged across the canvas)
- *Source* 1992 Mark Francis (A pattern of organic shapes like sperm. It appears like a photographic image from a microscope)
- *Dry Table* 1991 Grenville Davey (An intriguing sculpture, too high to be a table, kidney-shaped like a surgical tray)

Contemporary Art

CONTEMPORARY ART AT THE TATE

Contemporary art forms only a small part of the Gallery's displays and such shows last no longer than four months. Because of the size and role of the Tate Gallery, it usually only displays and purchases the work of established artists.

- The Turner Prize – Each year four artists under fifty are shortlisted for the Prize, and examples of their work are displayed in the autumn.
- Major exhibitions – Once a year, usually in the summer, there is an exhibition of work by a living artist or artists, either retrospective or thematic.
- Special Displays of the Collection – Thematic displays sometimes include contemporary art and recent acquisitions.
- Art Now – This room showcases the work of young, more experimental artists.

THE CONTEMPORARY ART WORLD

There are estimated to be thirty-five thousand professional artists working in Great Britain alone, ranging from the traditional and commercial to the most avant garde, displaying their work in over two thousand exhibition spaces ranging from large galleries like the Tate or the Whitechapel Art Gallery to alternative spaces and community centres.

Many factors have contributed to changing the languages and functions of art over the twentieth century. These factors include the trauma of world wars and new forms of communication and electronic imaging.

Contemporary art is being produced now, and so reflects issues of our time and makes use of the great variety of visual media currently available.

Many artists no longer seek to produce beautiful or skilful objects within narrow definitions of what was traditionally accepted as art. They rather seek to challenge how we see and understand the world, using the media that they feel is most resonant or immediate for the purpose. This might involve using traditional techniques, or instead include a variety of media such as food, old clothes, video, sound or organising an event. These artists borrow from many sources outside the conventions of fine art, such as psychology, science or popular culture. The art world validates certain objects as art and there is little purpose in asking 'is it art?'. A more rewarding question is 'what does this mean to me?'

It is problematic to talk of a distinctively 'British' art, especially as Britain becomes more culturally diverse. There has always been a degree of exchange between artists of different countries, but the expansion of air travel, mass media and the international art market has resulted in artists being open to influences from Europe, America and beyond. It is important for British art to be seen in a global context.

FEATURES OF CONTEMPORARY ART

Using new media
Many artists now incorporate a wide range of media into their work, such as:

READY-MADE OR FOUND OBJECTS
Artists such as Picasso and Duchamp were using found objects as early as 1913 and contemporary artists carry on this tradition.
- *Forms without Life* 1991 Damien Hirst (Real shells in a shop or museum display cabinet)
- *Untitled (Air Bed II)* 1992 Rachel Whiteread (A rubber cast of a bed, with associations of sex, sleep and death)
- *Cold Dark Matter: An Exploded View* 1991 Cornelia Parker (An exploded garden shed, its particles suspended)

FOOD
Artists have used real food at least since the 1960s. For example, Joseph Beuys used margarine in *Fat Battery* 1963, suggesting fuel and the stuff of survival.
- *Bed* 1980–1 Anthony Gormley (A mattress of wax-soaked white bread slices imprinted with a life-size body in two halves)

FILM AND VIDEO
Film has been arguably the most ubiquitous and effective visual medium of the twentieth century so it is no surprise that fine art has appropriated it. Film is used in innovative ways for example, by projecting images into sculptural installations.
- *Good Boy Bad Boy* 1985 Bruce Nauman
- *The Most Beautiful Thing I've Ever Seen* 1995 Tony Oursler

PHOTOGRAPHY
Once again, fine artists use this very direct medium that overlaps with popular culture.

- *A Sudden Gust of Wind (After Hokusai)* 1993 Jeff Wall (A photographic tribute to a Japanese print)

TEXTILES

Feminism has helped to broaden use of materials. Traditional feminine art was domestic, such as needlework. This has been appropriated into a contemporary art of ideas.
- *Erase* 1989 Cathy de Monchaux
- *Virgin Shroud* 1993 Dorothy Cross

USING, AND ABOUT, THE BODY

The body was once thought a functional vessel for the soul. Now it is seen as the 'be-all and end-all'. It is the place where our intimate selves are made public and visible.
- *A Case for an Angel III* 1990 Anthony Gormley (Cast from the artist's own body)
- *Self-Portrait (Back no.16)* 1992 John Coplans (The artist's own hairy back in close up)
- *Enfleshings* 1989 Helen Chadwick (Pretty, or disgusting, meat)

INSTALLATIONS

Art now is made less for private consumption than for public sites such as galleries. Artists use a range of materials to create installations which respond to or fill such spaces. They can have a strong, holistic impact a bit like walking into a stranger's home.
- *Cell (Eyes and Mirrors)* 1989–93 Louise Bourgeois (Memories of her childhood home, playing out the 'psychosexual drama of the house')

An Art of Ideas

POLITICAL

Some contemporary artists use metaphor, humour and imagination to make resonant statements about political situations.
- *The state* 1993 Richard Hamilton (Oppression in Northern Ireland)
- *Lilith* 1987–9 Anselm Kiefer (The breakdown of cities)
- *Counterpane* 1987–8 Rita Donagh (Lament for tragedy of Irish history)

CONCEPTUAL

Conceptual art makes the viewer question the whole idea of art. It sometimes poses a concept in the place of a material object or image. It sometimes uses language to record events or thought processes.
- *Monument* 1980–1 Susan Hiller (A park bench, photographs of a memorial and a tape of the artist talking)

HUMAN THEMES

These are often ideas or images which are highly personal to the artist or specific to his/her culture, but universally relevant.
- *The Reserve of Dead Swiss* 1990 Christian Boltanski (Rows of photographs of people now dead. A modern *memento mori* – reminder of our mortality)
- *Nantes Triptych* 1992 Bill Viola (The birth of a child, the death of the artist's mother and a man spread Christ-like falling through water. The film is experienced as a large triptych in a darkened room)
- *Ataxia – Aids Is Fun* 1993 Derek Jarman

PLURALISTIC

Contemporary art does not reflect a single authoritative standpoint or cultural identity, but different voices are heard.
- *The Enclosure of Sanctity* 1992–3 Shirazeh Houshiary (Geometrical forms relating to Sufi mysticism)
- *Head* 1995 Tony Bevan (A raw, powerful image from a black artist)
- *Bismullah* 1988 Rasheed Araeen

SOME QUESTIONS TO ASK ABOUT ANY CONTEMPORARY WORK

How is it displayed? Do you think the artist was involved in decisions about how to display it? How does it interact with the space it is displayed in?
What devices are used to interact with the viewer? (Does it attract my attention with sound? Do I have to walk round it? Is it on a large scale? Is it shocking?)
Is it made with traditional or innovative techniques or materials? How do these relate to its possible meanings?
Are connections made to the contemporary world or does it look in to the world of art?
What can you see in it? What does it mean to you?

FURTHER IDEAS

Visit the annual Turner Prize display and debate who should win. Make connections with works in the permanent collection. Set up your own alternative selection of four artists, displaying reproductions of their work for everyone to vote on.
Can competition be applied to art?

Materials and Techniques

This section considers how artists translate what they have seen, felt, remembered or imagined into a physical object – a work of art. The term 'work' implies both the intellectual and physical effort involved in its making and the effect (the way it works) on the viewer. Looking at the finished work in a gallery it is easy to forget that it began as a selection of raw materials that an artist worked on with tools and techniques.

Francis Bacon saw the artist's task as 'to make idea and technique inseparable'. In creating a painting, 'every movement of the brush on canvas alters the shape and implication of the image'. For him 'real painting' involved 'a mysterious and continuous struggle with chance … taking advantage of what happens when you splash the stuff down'.

By closely examining a work of art we can discover something of how it was made and in turn come to appreciate how making and meaning are closely related.

From such an analysis, revealing connections between techniques and meaning, you are better informed to construct a critical and artistic response.

MATERIALS

Painting

Most of the paintings displayed in the Tate Gallery were made with oil paints. Before the use of oil-based paints becaame widespread in the sixteenth century, fresco and tempera were mainly used. The physical properties of these earlier media lent themselves to flat decorative designs. Such medieval stylised forms lingered on in some Tudor oil paintings such the *The Cholmondeley Ladies c.*1600 British School.

John Bettes's portrait *Man in a Black Cap* 1545 is an early example of the use of oil paints and the influence of the work of Holbein in this medium. The longer drying time of oil and range of consistency from thick opaque impasto to thin transparent glazes made it possible to create a new, more illusionistically real imagery. Look at the subtle skin tones in this portrait and the marks used to suggest the tangled beard and soft fur.

John Berger in his book *Ways of Seeing* suggests oil painting 'as an art form was not born until there was a need … to express a particular view of life for which the techniques of tempera or fresco were inadequate'. He goes on to say:

> What distinguishes oil painting from any other form of painting is its special ability to render the tangibility, the texture, the lustre, the solidity of what it depicts. It defines the real as that which you can put your hands on.
>
> Although its painted images are two-dimensional, its potential of illusionism is far greater than that of sculpture, for it can suggest objects possessing colour, texture and temperature, filling a space and, by implication, filling the entire world.

Oil paint is formed by grinding a coloured, powdered pigment into a purified oil such as linseed, walnut or poppy oils. For many thousands of years artists had used coloured earth pigments – the ochres, umbers and blacks. Other pigments were added to these over the centuries coming from many parts of the world, such as Cinnabar red from Egypt, Tyrian purple from Roman whelk shells and ultramarine blue from Middle Eastern lapiz lazuli. The vast array of colours we know today however, were not invented until the expansion of chemical and dyeing industries in the 19th century. Turner enthusiastically used many of these new colours especially the whole range of vibrant yellows we find in his sun-filled landscapes.

The Pre-Raphaelites also used the new jewel-like colours, shocking those used to the subdued tones of traditional academic art.

Today we buy paints ready mixed, but up until the nineteenth century most artists would mix their own colours. Whilst some pigments are very stable, others may change over time. In many Renaissance paintings foliage may appear black where it was once bright leaf green. Works on paper, such as watercolours and prints are doubly vulnerable due to light discolouring the paper as well as fading the colours. This is why rooms displaying such works may have dimmed lighting.
- *A Man in a Black Cap* 1545 John Bettes
  (The murky background to this portrait was originally a rich blue. Made from smalt, a translucent glass pigment, it has badly faded and reacted with the underpainting)

Painters have also used varnish to protect a finished painting, but over time this often yellowed and darkened, giving a sooty appearance to once sparkling colours. It is the job of the Conservation Department to tackle these problems and others concerned with damage, deterioration and preservation.

Sculpture

Today sculptors use a vast range of materials from dead cows to video, each reflecting a different language of experience. Traditionally sculptors used marble, wood, clay or cast bronze.

Edgar Degas, the French Impressionist painter, was also a sculptor. His sculptures of dancers were modelled in wax, a material that enabled him to build up the forms quickly and capture the movement of a dancer. What changes in effect do you think took place when these were later cast into hard bronze?

David Smith, the American sculptor, began making forged and welded iron sculptures in the 1930s, often incorporating discarded tools and farm implements. These have a muscular simplicity that has more to do with the blacksmith's forge than the traditional sculptor's practice.

Looking at any examples, one each of a painted and a sculpted figure, what are the qualities and limitations of each medium in representing a figure?

TOOLS AND TECHNIQUES

Painting

Artists apply paint with a variety of brushes or a palette knife, rag or many other means. Each tool and the way it is used will produce a characteristic range of marks.

- *Queen Elizabeth I c.1575* attributed to Nicholas Hilliard (Hilliard was a great miniature painter, so when he painted the Queen's elegant jewellery and embroidery he used very fine brushes to capture the details)
- *Yellow Islands* 1954 Jackson Pollock (Pollock, the American Abstract Expressionist, often dripped household paint direct from a tin or flicked it in dramatic arcs using a stick coated in fluid paint. He would lay a large unstretched canvas on the floor and work from all four sides. He said 'I feel nearer, more a part of the painting since this way I can walk around it … and literally be in the painting'. This technique produces a distinct sense of space and composition – the 'all-over' effect, and sense of rhythm and frozen energy in the skeins of paint)

Sculpture

The tools and procedures used for modelling clay produce very different results to those used to produce a carving. It was usual to cast modelled sculptures into more durable materials such as bronze. If you look closely at a cast bronze by Degas, Rodin or Epstein you can see the way the original clay forms were created by hand, their textures and rhythms. In comparison, look at any marble or wood carving to find traces of the chisel and file marks. Notice how certain parts have been honed to a smooth finish.

There may also be a constructed sculpture on display, for example:
- *Head No.2 (Enlarged Version)* 1964 Naum Gabo
- *Cubi XIX* 1964 David Smith
- *Terra Incognita* 1968–82 Lothar Baumgarten
- *Night Movements* 1987–90 Anthony Caro

Such works have been assembled from prefabricated parts. Sometimes an artist may incorporate pre-existing or found objects or they may have been carefully shaped before assembly. The manner of construction depends on the weight and type of materials but they may be welded, tied, glued or even just leaning together.

FURTHER IDEAS

Consider the different qualities of space and volume in a constructed sculpture (as above) and those in a modelled or carved form, for example by Rodin.

Make drawings to deconstruct a constructed sculpture back to its separate elements.

WHERE ART IS PRODUCED

A gallery space is very different from the place in which the art work was initially made, and the place an artist works in will directly influence what is produced.

Painting

Most painters work in a studio or workshop of some kind. Even landscape painters such as Turner created their finished paintings in the comfort of a studio, working from sketches made from nature, often many years previous.

Looking at a historic British painting, such as *Giovanna Baccelli* 1782 by Thomas Gainsborough, try reconstructing what happened in the studio. Was the figure actually posed against the background shown or painted separately? Is the background drawn from observation of a real place or invented?

In the late nineteenth century the Impressionists began working outdoors direct from nature, frequently completing a painting in a single sitting. This immediate contact with the scene marked a shift from classically composed paintings toward a concern to capture the fleeting qualities of light and everyday activity.

- *Claude Monet Painting at the Edge of a Wood* c.1887 John Singer Sargent

Sculpture

Many modern sculptors work in converted industrial spaces, using engineering tools and processes. Artists such as Rodin in the nineteenth century and Henry Moore in this century would fashion small models or maquettes which assistants would then enlarge, the artist then applying the finishing touches. Both these sculptors produced large public sculptures requiring many technical assistants, heavy machinery and a large workshop.

John Singer Sargent **Claude Monet Painting at the Edge of a Wood** *c*.1887

ORIGINALS AND COPIES

One of the qualities many people value in a work of art is authenticity but not all works of art are unique. There is a long tradition of sculptors producing an edition of casts from an original. The Degas bronzes of dancers are an example of this. Similarly, print makers will produce an edition of a print from a handful to many hundreds.

- *Marilyn Diptych* 1962 Andy Warhol (This work was one of a large series produced using photo-silkscreen images of Marilyn Monroe. Warhol had a team of assistants turning out dozens of works a day under his supervision.)

As long as the artist oversees these activities we can assume the work is still authentic, but what if it is produced by others at a later date? The bronze dancers were produced from the originals after Degas's death. The large Gabo *Head No.2* (illustrated on p.9) was greatly enlarged in 1964 from a small work produced nearly fifty years previously.

FURTHER IDEAS

Select a work of art that interests you. Make notes and sketches of:
- the materials used – their size, character and limitations
- the way the artwork has been physically constructed
- the textures and marks used – brushstrokes, chisel marks, etc
- possible tools and techniques used to produce the work

Relate these observations to the subject matter and meanings communicated by the art work. To what extent are 'idea and technique inseparable'?

Making your Booking

Bookings must be made by telephone so that details can be discussed. A letter or message cannot be accepted as a booking. If you represent an adult education group telephone the Information Office on 0171-887 8734. If you represent a school, college or community group telephone Tate Education on 0171-887 8767.

Gallery talks are very popular with school and college (pre-degree) groups. Such groups need to book at least four months in advance.

Community groups can book nearer the time of the event, can negotiate for it to take place at weekends or at any time of the day, within the opening hours of 10.00 – 17.50.

Be ready with the following facts when you phone: a range of dates, your full address and telephone number, group size. The content can be discussed at a later date.

Essential information for planning
- Supervision of children under sixteen is required at all times
- The maximum length of visit for a group is three hours
- The maximum group size is sixty
- There are group lunch and cloakroom facilities but these are limited to certain groups booked well in advance

Facilities for people with disabilities
Please let us know if there are wheelchair users so that we can advise you about parking and access routes.

Touch tours of sculptures are available for people with visual impairment. We are always happy to discuss ways in which we can provide for your particular needs.

Further resources
- Labels by each work explain key facts and ideas
- Notes and packs for most major exhibitions are available for booked groups
- The audio guide *TateInform* provides spoken commentaries. Please telephone 0181 747 3744 for group bookings and prices
- A wide range of broadsheets, catalogues, companion guides and books are for sale in the shop or by mail. Please telephone 0171 887 8870
- Images for use outside the Gallery, such as slides and postcards

Preparing first-time visitors
What is an art gallery? Is it like a church, a museum, a department store? The Tate Gallery exists both to collect and protect art works and to show and explain them to visitors.

'You'd have thought they'd have the Mona Lisa in there, wouldn't you? My grandad's got one!' [ten-year-old on leaving the Tate Gallery]. Make clear that these works are *original* and valuable, compared to reproductions. Explore why you are visiting to see the real thing.

Why can't we touch? The sweat in your hands contains acids which damage pictures and sculptures. This damage can only be seen under a microscope but in time the work of art will deteriorate.

The group may need some introduction to vocabulary and types of art, e.g. 'portrait', 'sculpture' (not always 'statue') and 'scale' (a more accurate word than 'size').

Beware of over-preparing. Retain the magic and the element of surprise. Try to avoid giving loaded preconceptions – about the value of modern art, for example – which might prevent a fresh discovery of the Tate's collections.

IF YOU ARE HAVING A GALLERY TALK OR A WORKSHOP

A Gallery Talk:
- Lasts one hour
- Looks at four or five works
- Takes place entirely in the galleries
- Balances open questions with information

- Adapts the content and language level to the needs of the group
- Makes connections, comparing and contrasting works of art
- Includes, if appropriate, simple word or memory games and stimulus of the imagination

A Gallery Workshop:
- Lasts ninety minutes
- Looks at five or six works
- Takes places entirely in the galleries
- Extends the experience of looking and talking with 'clean' practical or language activities

Structuring the visit around an event

Arrive fifteen minutes (but ideally no longer than that) before the visit is due to start. This allows enough time to be greeted, to use the toilets and to put bags away.

Leave about thirty to sixty minutes afterwards for further exploration of the Gallery, for sketching and for visiting the shop.

If you are having a ninety minute workshop, it is not advisable to plan another substantial activity to do at the Tate Gallery on the same visit.

Be aware that gallery educators cannot guarantee beforehand the works that will be seen in an event.

Doing your own teaching

We recommend a preliminary visit as displays are regularly changed. If you wish to look at specific works of art with your group, check at the Information Desk that they will be on display when your group intend to visit.

Most groups of young people come between the hours of 10.00 and 13.00. If the members of your group are over eighteen years old or you want to lecture on specific works, we would advise you to come in the afternoon.

If you want to conduct a group talk, bear in mind the following:
- Ideally, talk to fewer than twenty-five people
- The group is best seated, on the floor or with the available stools
- Badged Tate speakers have priority so you may be asked to move from an area after a reasonable amount of time
- You will not be able to speak to a group larger than six in a paying exhibition

Galleries can be exciting but very tiring. Focus on achievable aims. It is not a good idea to plan a trail or tour which covers the whole Gallery. Focus on one theme, one or two rooms or compare one period to another.

Works of art act as an excellent stimulus for discussion. If you are writing task sheets allow opportunities for pairs or groups to talk to each other, based on what they see. Collecting facts from the labels can be useful to inform looking but should not dominate the visit.

Although groups should be asked to be respectful of other visitors, galleries are social places and it is fine to talk.

Recording the visit

You can try using a tape recorder to record discussions and responses, but remember that the Gallery is often busy.

Only a fraction of the works you see will be available as postcards. Bring a camera to record favourite works, but remember that flash and tripods cannot be used.

Use a sketchbook – see the section 'Drawing in the Gallery' for ideas.

Researching Personal Studies

This section is written for GCSE, GNVQ and A level students who may wish to use the Tate to resource personal studies in art and art history.

For any enquiries about works on display telephone the Information Office on 0171 887 8726

DOES YOUR TOPIC FIT THE TATE'S COLLECTIONS?

In London, the Tate's displays include:

Historic British Collection
- Tudor portraits
- Sixteenth and seventeenth-century portraits and some landscapes
- Eighteenth-century paintings by Hogarth, Reynolds, Gainsborough, Stubbs, etc.
- William Blake
- Constable and other landscape artists
- Hundreds of paintings and works on paper by J.M.W. Turner
- Victorian painters including Pre-Raphaelites
- Late nineteenth-century painters such as Sargent, Steer, Whistler

Modern Collection
- Some Impressionist and Post-Impressionist paintings (the best places to see these, however, are the National Gallery and the Courtauld Institute)
- Sculptors, including Rodin, Moore, Caro, Hepworth
- British twentieth-century artists, such as Bacon, Freud, Spencer and Gwen John
- European Modernists such as Picasso, Kandinsky, Boccioni, Dalí
- Abstract Expressionists such as Rothko and Pollock
- British, European and American contemporary art

Display changes
The art listed above is shown in the thirty rooms of *New Displays*, which are arranged chronologically but do not rigidly define art historical movements. Most rooms change once a year, but some change up to four times a year.

Exhibitions
There are many special displays and exhibitions throughout the year, which last two to four months. Keep looking at art listings or telephone the Information Office to find out what is coming up.

From 2000
British art from the Tudors to the present day will be on show in the new Tate Gallery of British Art at Millbank. International modern art from 1900 onwards will be shown in the new Tate Gallery of Modern Art at Bankside.

Gaps in the Tate Gallery Collection
It does not own any design, decorative art or non-Western art.

It does not own European art that is not modern. This means there is very little religious art.

Although it does own Pop art, it is not often on show in London.

It owns a very small number of works by the following artists: Cézanne, Chagall, van Gogh, Gauguin, Klee, Gustav Klimt.

It does not own work by Frida Kahlo or Georgia O'Keefe.

Bear in mind that the Tate in London only has room to show a small percentage of its collection. Many Tate works, especially the most popular, go out on loan to other exhibitions or galleries. They may also be seen at Tate Gallery St Ives or Tate Gallery Liverpool. The rest will be in store or in conservation (being cleaned or repaired).

The easiest topics to do at the Tate
Thematic topics such as landscape, animals, representations of women.

The following artists are almost always on display: Turner, Constable, Pre-Raphaelites, Surrealists, Futurists, Picasso, British figurative artists.

WRITING TO TATE EDUCATION

The main function of gallery education staff is to help visitors engage with works of art on display. We receive around a hundred enquiries per month from students so there is a limit to the attention we can offer each of them.

How can we help?
- We can inform you about any event at the Tate relevant to your chosen topic
- We can send you reading lists on some artists in the Tate's collection
- We can send you worksheets, catalogue entries or teacher's notes if we happen to have some relevant to your needs
- We organise tutorial days for you to have one-to-one help

How can't we help?
- We cannot answer questionnaires
- We cannot give opinions on your essay
- We cannot answer questions about works not owned by the Tate Gallery
- We cannot give general information on a very broad issue
- We cannot arrange interviews with artists and curators

RESOURCES FOR RESEARCH

The following resources are available to help with research:
- There are extended captions by each work
- You can consult files on all the Tate's artists and works behind the Information Desk
- The Tate shop sells postcards and gallery guides at reasonable prices
- You can take a *TateInform* recorded tour, where you listen to information on your choice of a wide selection of works
- There are three or four daily guided tours, no need to book

Note The Tate Library and Archive are only open to professional researchers.

The stores have now moved to a building away from the Gallery. This means that access to works not on display is limited.

FIRST STEPS IN PLANNING YOUR PROJECT

If you must prove that you have seen actual art-works, then focus your study primarily around those objects, rather than basing it entirely on what you have read. Use your reading to inform and support your looking.

It is better to start with objects you know you can experience first hand, if work by your favourite artists can only be found in books.

Use a local resource. Get into the habit of visiting galleries, museums, sculpture parks, and looking at the design of buildings and objects everywhere you go. The best way to understand an art object is to spend time with it and to revisit it.

If you choose a work owned by the Tate Gallery, find out if it is on display, for example by making a preparatory visit. At the time of writing *New Displays* for each year are complete in May/June, then, starting with the oldest art first, begin to change again in December. So the best times to do your looking are in the summer and autumn. Ask at the Information Desk how long your chosen work(s) will be on display.

GETTING THE MOST OUT OF YOUR VISIT

Focus on a small number of works, spending time with them

Make *connections* and comparisons with other works on display

Note down your *personal responses first*. What questions come to mind, what leaves you curious? Then use the wall texts and captions to find out more.

Be aware of the *gallery context*. This will help you prove that you have seen the actual art work, by providing information that could not have been gained otherwise. Where and how are these works displayed? Are they meant to be in a gallery? Do they look important in the room? How are they framed?

Always have a *purpose for any sketch*, not just to record its appearance. For example use your sketches to help you explore some of these questions below.

Prepare questions to ask before seeing your chosen object(s)

What is it?

Where is it?

How do you think it was made?

What is it made from?

What scale is it?

When do you think it was made?

For whom do you think it was made?

How realistic is it?

What shapes, colours, lines, patterns, textures, details, symbols can you see?

How is the space organised?

Do your eyes travel into an imagined space or do they stay on the surface?

What is the best viewpoint? Is it close up or distant, from below or at eye level?

If it is a sculpture, is it meant to be seen from the back, front or side, or all round?

What is it communicating?

How does its material or method relate to its meaning?

What does it mean to you? What does it remind you of?

What words best describe its mood?

Drawing in the Gallery

Sketchbooks are useful for responding to real artworks. As you are out and about, you need to collect and keep together a lot of visual and verbal information. A sketchbook helps record your progress and thoughts over time. You are also free to use your own personal style to respond to, and make sense of, what you see. You do not need to worry about making perfect or finished drawings.

Using a sketchbook to make visual notes can focus your mind to unravel what you see. Looking at art works can be bewildering and tiring. It can be hard to really concentrate on one work for a long time, even though you can gain more from spending time with just a few works.

Alternatively use paper on a clipboard or portfolio. It is also possible to draw on larger sheets on the floor. But note that the Gallery can be very crowded, so you should not lie flat or take up too much room.

MATERIALS

What do you need?
Any or all of these:
A drawing pen
Pencils, soft and hard
Coloured crayons
Felt tips (used with care)
Graphite or hard charcoal pencils (used with care)
Stapler or Pritstick

These materials cannot be used in the Gallery for safety reasons:
Paints
Charcoal
Fixative spray
Pastels
Ink bottles

Try to choose materials that are sympathetic to the object you are studying. In general you will not be able to use the identical materials as in the original art work but in any case your time is not best used trying to make a copy.

SOME IDEAS

For the record
Annotation is a good way to get down a general impression of your chosen work. Briefly sketch it, mapping the whole composition and key features. Write notes about it, pointing out aspects you cannot easily draw such as the colour or the texture of paint.

Look at the Gallery
Make notes and sketches on the arrangement of works in a room. What do artworks have in common? Consider the relative sizes of works. What are the decor, architecture, atmosphere and lighting like?

Viewpoints
Look at the art work from different angles and distances. How does this affect your experience of it? If it is three-dimensional is there an ideal viewpoint or are you supposed to move around it? If it is a painting try plotting the compositional devices which draw your eye around the flat surface or into any illusory space represented.

Memory Games
Look at the work for a few moments. Turn right round and draw what you remember. Or look, turn away and write a description. When you look back see what you have missed. An artist needs a sharp visual memory – when you get home try drawing from memory an image that really interested you.

Details
Randomly select small areas of a painting or sculpture in order to examine and draw the lines, brushstrokes, chisel marks or textures. Useful tools for this are a magnifying glass or a viewfinder. (Don't get so close that you touch!)

In the Picture
Choose a portrait or a figurative art work. Add to or replace one of the figures with your own face. Do not make it like a cartoon but try to use the style of the artist. Look hard at the clothes, the body shape and what is in the background.

Transform it

Make a sketch of your chosen work but change elements to explore their function. For example, take out particular objects or shapes, add more shadow or remove shading, soften hard edges, make soft shapes angular, make a realistic image abstract …

Composition

Make diagrams to analyse significant directional lines and shapes, the negative spaces between shapes, the highlights and focal points. Map how your eye moves.

Beyond the Frame

If you think of the art work as a frozen moment in time, try drawing what had happened before this moment and what may happen next. The art work has been composed to be just that size, but try extending it, imagining what lies beyond the frame.

More Ideas for the Gallery

USING THE DISPLAYS

In one room, working in small groups or pairs, think of one-word responses to these questions: What is the feeling of the whole room (look beyond the art)? What do all the art works have in common? What is the theme or key idea behind this selection of art works?

Which work did you notice first? Which work(s) didn't you notice at all?

Which work in this room would you like to take home with you and why? Which should have been left behind in the stores?

Make connections. Can you find any links between any two of the works of art? For example, the same figure or face, the same colours, the same mood?

Opposites. Find any two works which you think are the most opposite.

You could go on to make a whole collection of opposites or connections. You could also use sketching to record and explore these similarities or differences.

Working with just two or three works, in pairs discuss what they tell us about the time they were made in.

WORDS: DESCRIPTIVE OR CREATIVE

A good starting point may be to list colours, shapes, textures, symbols and moods you associate with the art work. Compare two works, listing what is similar and what is different. You may want to use opposite words like real/imaginary, soft/hard, light/dark, excited/calm. Perhaps imagine what you can smell, taste or hear, or what temperature or weather you associate with the work?

Try rewriting the given label based on what the art work means to you personally or using the right language for a particular reader.

INTERVIEW A WORK OF ART

This helps you make imaginative leaps. It works well with a portrait or figurative sculpure, but be daring and try it with a more abstract work.

What is the name given to you by the person who made you? (Title)
What do you prefer to be called?
When were you born?
Do you feel old or young?
What is your star sign?
Are you an indoors type or an outdoors type?
What is your favourite colour?
What is your motto or favourite saying?
If you could change anything about yourself what would it be?
Do you mind if I find your best view and take a sketch?

These interviews could be made into a 'Hello at the Tate' magazine to share with others who could not visit.

DON'T TOUCH!

It is especially difficult for young children to look without touching. To deal with this necessity, explain why, then ask them to *touch with their eyes*.

Or, talk about what surfaces might feel like to touch.
Ask children to imagine that they are a really sensitive snail crawling slowly over it. What is the temperature? The texture? What does it remind you of? ('It feels like coal/cotton wool/nails down blackboards …').

Awaken the other senses. What does it smell, taste, sound like?

If you have the time to prepare you could bring in your own touchable objects, such as carved wood, or marble, cloth, paper or wax. Children could match the sensations to the different sculptures/objects. You could allow children to be fairly lateral in their matching.

VIEWPOINTS

Most works of art have an ideal viewpoint. Try to find it. Is it far away, close up, low down, looking from above, behind, sideways, directly in front? What is the worst viewpoint? Does it become distorted?

Does it actually make it more interesting if you see it from the viewpoint not intended?

Try changing the way your eyes work to get a different impression of the art work. For example squint or go cross-eyed. Cover part of it. Do you notice anything new?

Try this sketching game. In a group of three to ten people, all start a sketch from one viewpoint around a sculpture, then after two or three minutes, move to the next person's paper leaving your own behind, adding your interpretation to the same viewpoint.

MEMORY GAMES

Without talking, spend a minute to just look at a work of art, particularly one with a range of features or details.

Four variants:

- Everone is to turn away from the work. Each person lists as many things as they can remember seeing. The longest list wins
- Ask the group to close their eyes, then ask individuals to name one thing they can remember seeing, without repeating what others saw
- If you prefer to be less competitive, with any work of art, ask them to turn away to sketch what they saw. Everyone will have noticed different things and interpreted them in their personal way
- With figurative works. After looking, one or two people turn their backs and take up the pose and expression of figures in the work. They must not look back. The others give instructions on how they can achieve perfect mimicry. You could record this activity with a camera

BE A TIME-TRAVEL DETECTIVE

This works well with story pictures, for example, by Victorian artists.

These paintings were made in a different age. People then would know more easily what the artist meant. (To understand this, imagine a time traveller from two hundred years ago arriving in your living room to watch *Eastenders*.) Your mission is to work out what is going on in a picture. List all the clues you can see. What happened before the scene here, what happened just afterwards? Write it up as a detective's report.

THE SCULPTOR AND HIS CLAY

In small groups one child (or more) is the sculptor, the others are the clay which he or she models into interesting shapes, like those seen in any sculpture.

Using the body to develop a tangible understanding of sculpture, you can explore concepts of balance, mass, hollowness, distortion from naturalism and so on.

SOME VOCABULARY

This is not a complete vocabulary of art but provides definitions of some words that have been used in this pack or which may be confusing.

DO YOU SAY 'SIZE' OR 'SCALE'?

Size – use when you are discussing the actual dimensions of a work of art

Scale – a more useful word than size as it suggests a proportional relationship to surroundings and proportions within a work of art

THE LANGUAGE OF SCULPTURE

Three dimensional – 'In the round', having length, breadth and depth

Sculpture – Artworks which are 'in the round' or in relief

Statue – A three-dimensional heroic portrait

Relief – Moulding, carving or stamping-in so that the design stands out from the surface

Maquette – A model for a finished sculpture or design

Site specific – A work of art which is made or adapted especially for the place it is shown in

Installation – Every work of art is installed when it is put on display. But this term is used when the artwork cannot be defined as a painting or sculpture etc and when the artist is conscious of occupying and interacting with a space. It may consist of many parts, or use sound, light, film or smells

Patina – Surface finish

Carving – Cutting into a block of solid material

Modelling – Building up or manipulating materials such as wax or clay

Assembling – Bringing together different materials to form one piece

Casting – Pouring a molten material into a mould, then removing the mould to reveal a durable object. You can make several versions

DESCRIBING ART

Idealised – Transformed from ordinary to become perfect or typical

Aesthetic – Beautiful, tasteful. Also, making art for art's sake

Picturesque – The conventional way of picturing a place or landscape to be pleasing to the eye

Topographical – A precise, objective visual account of a building or place

Symbolic – Meanings communicated through visual signs, which stand for something other than what they are in themselves

Naturalistic – Representing nature or appearances realistically and in detail

Expressive – Using gestures, colours etc to convey emotions

Distorted – Exaggerating or transforming the appearance of things for expressive effect

Graphic – Descriptive or clearly drawn

Reduced – Toning down colours or simplifying shapes to calm the mood or clarify the design

Minimal – Reduced to the minimum; few colours and simple geometric shapes

Surreal – Literally 'beyond real'; strange or bizarre; irrational juxtapositions

THE LANGUAGE OF FORM

Composition – Arranging form, line, tone, colour, etc. to create effects, harmonies, movement

Form – Shapes and relationships between shapes

Focal point – Where your eye is drawn to, perhaps to a significant part of the image

Movement – Some artists aim to create an impression of movement, using directional lines for example

Foreground – In art which aims to create an illusion of depth, the foreground is that which seems to be nearest the viewer

Background – That in the distance, or behind a figure

Picture plane – The extreme front edge of this imaginary space, where the viewer enters the picture